Flower Gardening: A Primer

James W. Wilson

Flower Gardening: A Primer

VNR VAN NOSTRAND REINHOLD COMPANY
NEW YORK CINCINNATI TORONTO LONDON MELBOURNE

Flower Gardening: A Primer is dedicated to the seedsmen of North America, Japan and Europe with whom I have worked for the greater part of my adult life. In particular I wish to thank the seedsmen and garden editors who have assisted in authentication of this book:

Mrs. Isabel Zucker—
National Garden Bureau, Detroit, Mich.

Mr. Elmer Twedt—
Ferry-Morse Seed Co., San Juan Bautista, Calif.

Mr. David Lemon—
an associate of Mr. Twedt, formerly with Wisley Gardens, London, England

Mr. Gerald Burke—
The W. Atlee Burpee Co., Riverside, Calif.

Mrs. Zucker's help was invaluable; the book benefited not only from her long experience as a garden editor but also from her woman's viewpoint.

Numerous seedsmen graciously contributed photographs. The many beautiful old pen and ink sketches are reproduced from *Album Des Cliches* (circa 1911) with the permission of the venerable seed company, Vilmorin Andrieux & Cie., Paris, France. Hrand Hampikian, Landscape Architect, provided all of the photographs in Chapter 2. Peggy Yamagiwa is responsible for the instructive drawings throughout the book.

James W. Wilson

Van Nostrand Reinhold Company Regional Offices:
New York   Cincinnati   Chicago   Millbrae   Dallas

Van Nostrand Reinhold Company Foreign Offices:
London   Toronto   Melbourne

Copyright © 1970 by Litton Educational Publishing, Inc.
Library of Congress Catalog Card Number 70-110066

All rights reserved. No part of this work covered by the copyrights hereon may be reproduced or used in any form or by any means—graphic, electronic, or mechanical, including photocopying, recording, taping, or information storage and retrieval systems—without written permission of the publisher. Manufactured in the United States of America

Published by Van Nostrand Reinhold Company
450 West 33rd Street, New York, N.Y. 10001

Published simultaneously in Canada by
D. Van Nostrand Company (Canada), Ltd.

16 15 14 13 12 11 10 9 8 7 6 5 4 3 2 1

CONTENTS

	How to Use This Book	6
1	Classes of Plants	10
2	Planning a Flower Garden	12
3	Planting and Caring for a Garden	21
4	Tools and Equipment	30
5	Improving and Managing Your Soil	32
6	Controlling Natural Enemies	41
7	Quick Reference Charts of Plants	47
8	Annuals: Important Kinds Described in Detail	68
9	Perennials and Biennials: Important Kinds Described in Detail	94
	Glossary	111
	Index	116

HOW TO USE THIS BOOK

This book is for beginners in gardening—for the housewife who, kept close to home by children, needs the creative outlet of gardening and the morale boost that flowers can bring. It is for the husband who likes to express his love for his family by making the house and yard more beautiful and livable through do-it-yourself projects.

This book is for the family on a tight budget. It gives specific plans and step-by-step instructions for growing color with seeds, bulbs and small plants. You will enjoy reading the book because it is nontechnical. It assumes that you were exposed to no more than a smattering of botany or biology in school.

I would be enormously pleased to learn that you curled up one evening with the book and read through all or most of it. However, I realize that most beginning gardeners will use the book for answers to specific questions. You will have no problem in locating sections dealing with soils, fertilizers, pest controls, etc.; the Table of Contents is organized for easy reference. However, you will need to go one step further in locating information on specific flowers.

The garden flowers are organized first by the natural groups into which they are classified . . . annuals, biennials and perennials, bulbs, etc. The reason for this arrangement is that this is how they are sold in garden shops. Within the natural groups the flowers are listed alphabetically *by common name.* Many garden editors prefer to list plants by their Latin names for the sake of accuracy, and they have a point. However, I have observed that beginning gardeners have a friendlier feeling about flowers that they can call by their old-fashioned, often nostalgic or romantic names. As gardeners gain experience, they often learn the Latin names of flowers, and for this reason I have included the latest Latin nomenclature.

Look in the Index at the back of the book for the common name or Latin name of flowers. Important annuals, biennials and perennials are described in detail in the chapters following the Quick Reference Charts. To avoid making this book formidably long, the Tender Perennials, Spring Bulbs, Flowering Vines, and Water and Bog Plants are described only within their respective Quick Reference Charts.

The following capsule descriptions of the chapters in the book outline how the information therein can be of value to you:

CHAPTER 1
CLASSES OF PLANTS

If I were to name one chapter as "required reading," this would be it. For this reason the chapter has been kept short. Much of this book won't make sense unless you know the major natural groups of flowers. You may have encountered their names: annuals, perennials and biennials, etc. Chapter 1 explains the major differences between the groups, such as planting dates and season of bloom, and the meaning of these differences to gardeners.

CHAPTER 2 PLANNING A FLOWER GARDEN

Don't let the title intimidate you. Flower beds are easy to plan. Generally, three kinds of flowers will suffice to create an interesting floral effect. You can do a quick sketch on the back of an envelope before you go out to shop for seeds, bulbs or plants. It's when you get ambitious and decide to put in two or three flower beds that you need to give serious thought to color balance, continuity of bloom and gradations in height. But take heart; when you have lived to enjoy a few seasons in your garden, you no longer will need to draw elaborate plans, but can stand in front of a display of seeds or plants and pick out the ingredients of a first-class garden. If you are a beginner, however, a quick reading of Chapter 2 can save you the embarrassment of "goofs" like planting three-foot marigolds in front of one-foot zinnias.

CHAPTER 3 PLANTING AND CARING FOR A GARDEN

This is the "How To" chapter. Learning to garden by trial and error can be fun, but it can also be frustrating when you can't figure out why you failed. Chapter 3 condenses the author's gardening experience into a few rules that will enable you to plant flowers with the confident expectation that they will sprout and thrive. You would be amazed at how many gardeners never gain the confidence to try more than a few staple flowers. Usually, it is because they lack the curiosity to learn even the most basic laws of Nature. These timid souls never really get to feel that they are "tuned-in" to the seasons, to the small ecological islands in their home grounds, or to the personalities of the flowers they grow. They treat flowers like outdoor furniture.

Within one season you can begin regarding Nature as an ally except when, by ignorance or oversight, you run counter to her laws in your gardening efforts.

CHAPTER 4 TOOLS AND EQUIPMENT

You don't have to buy out the neighborhood hardware store to prepare, plant and care for a flower bed. Yet, you can't do it with your bare hands. Believe it or not, a shovel, rake and trowel will see you through your first gardening season. You will have to resist the temptation to buy gadgets before you gain experience in gardening. Many of the gadgets were invented by men who assume that the tool will be eagerly accepted by the gardening market. Yet, they· overlook the fact that no two individuals are constructed alike, nor do they push, pull, reach, grip or lift in the same way. Consequently, some of the centuries-old, dirt-simple designs for hand tools still in use work better than modern gadgets. Remember, if you get stuck for a tool for a special job, consider renting. Why tie up money in expensive tools when you can rent everything from power posthole diggers to electric hedge shears?

CHAPTER 5 IMPROVING AND MANAGING YOUR SOIL

You just might turn out to be one of those fortunate souls who can grow lovely flowers by doing little more than planting seeds or bulbs and watering them when the spirit moves you. But, as is often the case, your soil may be stubborn about cooperating in your creative endeavors. You can't beat it into doing your will. Managing garden soil is much like getting along with a small child; you have to make an effort to understand it and then you have to watch its responses carefully to know whether you are treating it in the best way to make it do your will.

If you grew up in an apartment or in a home with a small yard where you had little opportunity to dig in the soil, you will enjoy reading this chapter. I cannot describe the primitive satisfaction that goes with turning over soil that your efforts can make bountiful. You will just have to go through the experience yourself.

CHAPTER 6 CONTROLLING NATURAL ENEMIES

I have had other garden editors

caution me not to dwell on the problems that can beset gardeners for fear of frightening away beginners. Well, I have more faith in the willingness of the beginner to accept reality. If having your own garden means enough to you for you to read books on the subject, then you are ready to accept a little bitterweed with your sweet alyssum.

Insects, plant diseases (not communicable to humans) and weeds are a fact of life in your garden. They rarely become a serious problem, thank heaven, but when they do you will need help. You will probably go to the garden store for the appropriate chemicals to control the problem. When you go, take a sample of the affected plant with you. Go to a nurseryman who has been doing business in your community for some time and let him recommend the most effective control.

Chapter 6 won't make you an expert on creepy-crawlies and all the blights that can befall buttercups, but it will help you decide whether you are confronted with a plant disease, an insect, or a nutritional deficiency.

CHAPTER 7 QUICK REFERENCE CHARTS OF PLANTS

You'll find the vital statistics of a great many flowers here. The popular kinds are indicated with an asterisk. In a way, this is unfair to a great many deserving but overlooked flowers, yet, if you stick to the popular kinds you will find them versatile and easy to grow. No one has a reasonable explanation for the fact that a certain flower may be quite popular in one town while in another town no more than an hour's drive away, other flowers are preferred. Mass-marketed plants are generally made up of only a few kinds of flowers and this is steadily decreasing the frequency with which one sees the equally beautiful but less-promoted species.

Here's how to use the Quick Reference Charts to plan a flower garden. Let's assume, for example, that you want a summer-blooming garden of soft colors—perhaps in white, rose-pink and silvery-blue, and you want it for just one season. Turn to the charts for Annuals. They are one-season plants. Look for the customary three flowers: a low-growing edging flower, a medium-height bedding flower and a tall background flower.

Run your finger down the column of plant heights. There... alyssum is a low-grower and it comes in white. How about an 8- to 12-inch-high plant for filling in the center of the bed? Petunias certainly qualify, and their colors include several shades of pink. Okay so far.... Now for a tall blue background flower. There it is, way down the list, Salvia, 'Blue Bedder'; it's a delightful silvery-blue color.

Now, double check. Will all three be in bloom at the same time? Yes. Do they have the same preferences for sun or shade? Yes. Finally, are they easily obtainable? All are asterisked on the chart; you should have no trouble in finding seeds or plants. Now, turn to Chapter 8 to learn more about the three flowers you have chosen.

CHAPTER 8 ANNUALS: IMPORTANT KINDS DESCRIBED IN DETAIL

This chapter divides annuals into those that prefer cool weather and those that bloom best during summer months. This distinction is extremely important but is ignored by many books on gardening. For the most part, the list is made up from the bestsellers in seed displays and started plants, but it also contains several beautiful and deserving annuals that, for one reason or another, have never caught on.

CHAPTER 9 PERENNIALS AND BIENNIALS: IMPORTANT KINDS DESCRIBED IN DETAIL

These longer-lived plants should be chosen with extra care because they can come back year after year —the perennials from heavy roots and the biennials from natural reseeding. Some of the most extravagant advertising claims in all of horticulture are being made for certain perennials. The information in this chapter will help you to evaluate perennials and biennials objectively so that you will not be disappointed in what you buy.

The marigold is a common annual flower, available in many beautiful varieties. Photo: Bodger Seeds, Ltd.

1 CLASSES OF PLANTS

Like boating, golfing, or even knitting, gardening has its own terminology—convenient, accurate words that describe the specifics of gardening. Familiarity with basic gardening terms will simplify the reading of garden magazines and books, and can keep you from feeling like an outsider in conversations about gardening. Definitions of rather involved terms may be found in the glossary on page 111; other terms will be explained as they occur in the text. Let us review the classes of plants.

ANNUALS

Annuals are plants grown from seeds or cuttings that blossom, set seed, and die in one growing season.

Most are "summer annuals," which are planted in late spring or summer. They bloom all or part of the summer and die in the fall. The majority of summer annuals are frost sensitive, although some—petunias and marigolds, for example—survive moderate frosts.

"Cool-weather annuals" are those that are planted in the fall where winters are mild and in the early spring where winters are more severe. Plantings should be scheduled so that they bloom in cool weather, because hot weather causes them to set seed and die. This class is sometimes called "hardy annuals," which is somewhat misleading, since only a handful of cool-weather annuals are sufficiently frost-hardy to recover fully from twenty-degree weather. Examples of cool-weather annuals are California poppy, lobelia, nasturtium, pansy, and viola.

BIENNIALS

Plants grown from seeds or cuttings that form clumps the first year and do not flower until the second growing season are called "biennials."

Biennials are frost-hardy plants that live through severe winter weather as small, tough, young seedlings. With the warm days of the following spring the plants grow rapidly, and later in the season they are capped with blossoms. After blossoming, most biennial plants set seed and die. Examples: Canterbury bells, money plant (lunaria), and sweet William.

PERENNIALS

Perennials are comparatively long-lived plants grown either from seeds, stem or root cuttings, or other vegetative divisions. Examples; delphinium, phlox, and snow-in-summer.

Perennials vary considerably in hardiness to frost, but most live through long, hard winters when their tops may die but the roots survive to send up new sprouts each spring. Some, such as peonies, need the winter cold to bring on dormancy, or winter rest. (For this reason peonies don't flower well where winters are mild.)

The above description covers *hardy* perennials. There are also frost-tender plants that live outdoors for many years where winters are mild. These are called "tender perennials." Where winters are severe, tender perennials may be started indoors early to obtain a long season of bloom before frost kills the plants.

BULBS (INCLUDING CORMS, TUBERS, AND RHIZOMES)

In this book we shall not make much ado about the differences between bulbs, corms, tubers, and rhizomes. Briefly, bulbs have scales like lilies or layers like onions. Tulips are bulb flowers. Corms resemble bulbs but are solid, like gladiolus, with no scales or layers. Tubers of flowers such as dahlias are rough, torpedo or disc-shaped, fleshy, rootlike structures. Rhizomes (like iris) are fleshy, knotty, underground stems. All represent a dried remnant of a mother plant, a food-swollen bud, stem, or other part, capable of resuming growth when supplied with the proper conditions of air, water, temperature, etc.

WATER AND BOG PLANTS

These are plants that grow in ponds, pools, streams, containers of water, etc., or on marshy, waterlogged soil. Examples: Japanese iris, water lilies, marsh marigolds.

ROSES

The only woody plants included in this book are roses, because they are the most popular class of flowers in the United States and are a part of most garden plans. The subject of planting and care of roses is so specific, however, that no attempt will be made to cover it. Instead, roses will be included in garden planning only.

HOW TO USE FLOWERS

Edging flowers. Edgings are low-growing boundaries between walks and flower beds or between flower beds or borders and lawns.

Bedding flowers. These are low-to-medium-height flowers used to fill beds. Bedding flowers can be used in a single row to separate low-growing and tall flowers, or can be massed in a wide bed to add a dominant color effect to the landscape.

Background flowers. Waist-to-head-high flowers are often used behind bedding flowers to give height to a bed. Background flowers are also used to screen unsightly fences, structures or views.

Rock garden flowers. Generally this class includes low-growing plants that may creep or spread into a carpet. Also included are rosette-forming plants that can be chinked into crevices between rocks. A few taller plants that may be found growing among rocks in the wild—columbine, coral bells, etc.—also make good rock garden plants.

Groundcovers. Low-growing groundcover plants creep or spread and can take the place of lawns in areas with little or no foot traffic. Most groundcover plants are perennials; some bloom for several months each season. Only the ornamental groundcovers will be considered in this book—those with attractive blossoms or ornamental foliage.

Flowering vines. Clinging or twining plants that climb trees, fences, walls, posts or string have many uses. Clinging vines may need frequent tying up, although some adhere with sticky discs. Twining vines weave in and out or coil around supports and need little more than an occasional tucking in.

Amaranthus, or Love-lies-bleeding, is a somewhat exotic annual that lends interest to a border. Photo: Bodger Seeds, Ltd.

11

2 PLANNING A FLOWER GARDEN

To plant a garden without a plan is only for the thoroughly experienced gardener. To do so requires a thorough knowledge of flowers, practice, and a high degree of creative visualization. However, beginners can plant simple flower beds with little foreplanning.

Most gardeners, and especially landscape architects, "doodle" plans of their dream gardens. On a big sheet of paper they rough out a birdseye view of the building and lot and roughly sketch existing trees, shrubs, walls, walks, patios, garages, etc. They then mark the locations of view windows in the home and draw arrows from them to the areas most often seen. Finally, they locate places for strategic plantings. At this stage careful gardeners take a tape measure outdoors to check distances between major reference points, then redraw the roughed-out plot plan to scale. The easiest method is with graph paper, letting each square represent one or more square feet.

COMMON-SENSE CHECK LIST

Experience teaches one to review a common-sense check list before definitely deciding where to place flower beds. Here are points to consider.

Plant nutrients and water. Annuals, perennials, or bulbs can't compete with the strong, greedy roots of trees and large shrubs. It is not only the shade from the trees that causes flowers to grow poorly, it is also the competition for plant food and water. Therefore, don't plan a flower bed that extends under the "drip line" of a tree—the outermost spread of its branches—unless you can spare the time to feed and water the bed frequently.

Sun. The vast majority of plants prefer full sunlight or, at the least, direct sunlight for five or six hours daily. Don't plant sun-loving flowers in the shade; they will grow tall and lanky and will flower poorly.

Watering problems. Don't place flower or shrub beds at great distances from a hose bibb; dragging heavy lengths of hose around the garden can become a chore. If you place beds on sloping land, keep them out of the paths of natural drainage that could cause soil erosion. When making the beds, dig out the topsoil and pile it on the uphill side. Then, dig out some of the subsoil and pile it on the downhill side as "fill" to make the bed wider. Level the bed, roughly, and replace the topsoil. The front edge of the bed should be a little higher than back so that water can stand long enough to soak in.

Flooding. Is the bed in a low corner of the lot where rain water or melted snow can collect? Flooding is unhealthy and often fatal to flowers.

This border of perennials softens a 2-foot change in elevation from driveway to side yard. Planting includes delphiniums, lilies, penstemon and daylilies. The edging is of flowering sedum.

Relocate the bed or build it up so the soil level is at least six inches above the water line.

Size of beds. Stop and think about the problems of weeding. Are the beds too large? Are they too deep from front to back to be reached conveniently with a hoe? A depth of three to four feet is about the most that is workable. If the conformation of your yard dictates deeper beds, then plan "sneak paths" running parallel to the front edge. Such paths are screened from view by flowers, yet permit access to any part. Pave the paths with stepping stones so that you do not compact the soil between plants each time you use the path.

As a rule, one can weed and water two or three five-by-twenty-feet flower beds without cutting deeply into other leisure-time activities. Additional flower beds can be added if the extra work doesn't become a burden and cause one to resent the garden.

Background. What lies behind the flower bed? A fence or wall? Shrubs or trees? Such dominant masses influence air flow and sun reflection or shade. A fence or wall behind a west- or south-facing bed reflects sun and warms the surrounding air. Conversely, an east- or north-facing bed backed by a wall or fence is shaded much of the day and remains cooler.

YOUR OWN PLAN

Sketch the outlines of flower beds on the plot plan in the places you have set aside for them. Then, on separate sheets of paper, draw greatly enlarged outlines of the individual beds. Don't plant flowers only as a farmer plants corn, in straight rows. Free-form beds are generally more graceful than geometric designs. Also, beds around the perimeter of the yard or against the house are more pleasing to the eye than isolated beds laid down near the middle of the lawn. If you are courageous, plan a free-form "peninsula" bed jutting into the lawn. It will add depth and dimension to the view, providing that the size and shape are in keeping with the balance of the garden.

COST

Remarkable results can be obtained in a flower garden for an investment of from $1.00 to $10.00. Seeds provide the most economical route to color; $1.00 will buy four packets. $10.00 will give you a large flower garden complete with bulbs, fertilizer, and insecticide—enough for a whole season.

Young couples often do well to use the large, bushy, inexpensive annual flowers from seeds that serve beautifully as temporary shrubs until more permanent plant material can be afforded. Kochia, four o'clock, cleome (spiderflower), and tall red salvia are particularly good for this purpose.

Even if you are on a strict budget, politely decline most offers of cut-

Good use of a straight line shape where a narrow area would restrict a free-form bed. A small greenhouse is at back of property.

The foliage of perennials is interesting even when there are no blossoms. Perennial pinks at top of bed are just beginning to open.

Taller perennials such as delphiniums and lilies may require staking. Note the attraction of the eye to the entrance of the garden.

Eye-catching landscaping around a fieldstone barbecue grill. Note the excellent use of gray-foliaged dusty miller and white flowered matricaria (Feverfew). The mass of the flowers in the bed are fibrous-rooted begonias.

tings, plants, roots, and bulbs from well-meaning neighbors. Gift plants can introduce insects, diseases, and weeds to your garden. Further, if your neighbor has surplus plants, they are most likely of the common types that go through a population explosion each year, and he may be merely giving them away to keep from being inundated.

You can spend a great deal of money on gardening if you go in for the rare and unusual. Most families spend less than $100 yearly on their gardens, however, and this includes tools, fertilizer, flowers, and garden chemicals. Some top-notch gardeners spend considerably less.

HOW TO CHOOSE FLOWERS

There are so many flowers from which to choose that you will hardly know where to begin. A good place to start is with Chapters 8, 9, and 10—and in the better seed and plant catalogs. Even so, your first visit to a big seed display or a garden center with a large array of started plants may be a bewildering experience unless you go "list in hand." It is a rare home garden that can accommodate fifteen to twenty new kinds of flowers per season. To be sure, you can cram dozens of varieties into a small bed, but you create a hodgepodge, not a thing of beauty.

Annuals. Annuals are easy to plan because they are not as permanent as perennials or fall-planted bulbs. You can choose kinds that bloom all summer, or you can indicate a second and later "succession" planting to replace cool-weather annuals like candytuft or baby's breath after their blossoms are spent. In mild winter areas you can have annuals blooming twelve months of the year—in the northern tier of states, four months.

Bulbs. Next, choose your bulbs. Spring bulbs such as daffodils, hyacinths and crocus, can be considered as perennials because they come back year after year if you don't cut into them with a trowel or spade. (Where winters are short and mild, certain spring bulbs like tulips "run out" after a year or two from rapid splitting and multiplying, and flower size decreases.

While it is true that you can scatter and rake in seeds of summer flowers over your bulb beds, they are still primarily bulb beds, and you can't spade or cultivate deeply without damaging the bulbs. Perennials or biennials are satisfactory companions for spring-blooming bulbs, because they extend the blooming period and hide, or at least take one's attention away from, aging and yellowing bulb foliage.

Summer-planted bulbs, tubers, corms, or rhizomes, such as dahlias or cannas, call for special treatment. Often they look best when planted one kind to a bed or in large groups because of their dominant colors or hard-to-blend foliage.

Gently mounded shapes of medium-height perennial flowers blend with shrubbery in this pleasantly shaded garden.

Perennials and biennials. Choose your perennials and biennials last; see Chapter 10. These plants will be with you longer than annuals, so wait a while until you become acquainted with them. Perennials are usually planted in groups of three or more plants for color or height accents, unless they are big fellows like phlox or peonies, which are substantial enough to stand alone. Low-growing perennials can be used to edge beds. Don't underestimate the bushiness of large perennials; some grow wider than they are tall and may sprawl.

Roses. Modern hybrid tea and grandiflora roses are difficult to blend with other flowers or shrubs. The multifloras are easier to blend, but watch the thorns when you weed close to them. Most gardeners prefer to locate roses in special beds where plants can be given the necessary two to three feet separation necessary for easy access (four to five feet in California and Arizona). Concentrating roses in special beds, to the exclusion of other flowers, also allows gardeners to simplify the special chores involved in growing roses.

Most rosarians prefer to spread a mulch under their plants; however, such low-growing flowers as sweet alyssum establish rather easily among roses and can spread to serve as a flowering groundcover.

Tall climbing or pillar roses blend beautifully with all sorts of flowers, particularly perennials that bloom in early summer. Placed in the background and trained or supported into a graceful fountain form, the tall roses add a quaint touch. "Standard" or tree-form roses are often used in western and southern gardens, but are not hardy enough to take northern winters.

ARRANGING FLOWERS WITHIN BEDS

Stair-step heights. Ordinarily, you should not plant taller flowers in front of short ones. Arrange them in stair-step fashion as follows:

Front:
  edging flowers   4–12 inches high
Middle:
  medium-sized
  flowers   12–24 inches high
Rear:
  background
  flowers   24–48+ inches
                        high

Can you get by with only two of the three heights? Yes, but be sure to include medium-height bedding flowers in all plans. The lower-growing bedding plants billow attractively and thus hide bare lower stems —a valuable asset where space is at a premium. In narrow beds you can dispense with the larger, taller flowers and plant only one row of medium-height flowers.

Drifts. Long rows of edging, bedding and background flowers tend to look monotonous. Break the rows into irregular swatches or "drifts" of harmonizing colors three to five feet long. Where possible swirl the back-

This gardener fashioned a cool green glen in this corner with groundcovers and evergreens, then added geraniums and fibrous-rooted begonias for color.

Serpentine edging gives these beds of annuals great impact. Front, verbenas (next to tall lilies); back, dwarf marigolds, salvia, spiderflowers and a hedge of roses.

ground flowers out into the bedding plants for surprise effect or cut out a strip of edging and let bedding plants billow over the edge of the bed to soften its line.

Be generous. Don't skimp on space. In many cases only six to twelve flower plants can crowd a bed the size of a large kitchen table. Small, crowded beds have a patchwork look, since they lack the breadth to achieve unity through patterns of color. Beds of four by twenty feet, or larger, carry tremendous visual impact when planted with bright colors. Or, they can set a dignified mood if planted in pastel hues.

Companion colors. "What difference does it make if garden colors clash?" you may ask. "Isn't it Nature's way to display orange and pink cheek-by-jowl? The deciding factor is—do the clashing colors offend your taste? If not, let the colors run riot!

Here are some popular trios of harmonizing colors to help you work out edging, bedding, and background combinations:

SOFT PASTELS

white, light pink, blue; light blue, pale yellow, deep blue; lavender, white, violet; cream, mid-blue, rose pink

BRIGHTER COLORS

dark red, white, mid-blue; orange, white, scarlet; gold, blue, light yellow; lavender, orange, white

A cool pool of water lilies beneath a clump of birches. Pink petunias enliven the scene, along with dwarf polygonum groundcover.

Blue and light yellow are most useful as "blending" colors, surpassed only by silvery-gray foliage plants. White "separates" neighboring colors but is too forceful in effect to serve as a blending agent. Deep colors such as dark red, maroon, deep purple, mahogany, and plum must be used with discretion. These colors do not stand out against dark green foliage, particularly in the evening. Conversely, yellow and white flowers seem to glow when the stars come out. (Evening is the only time the compulsive weeder can enjoy his garden; he can see the flowers but not the weeds!) Brilliant color combinations should be placed way back in the garden to keep them from upstaging the gentle colors.

Then, there's the problem of

17

matching colors. Fortunately, bulbs come in separate colors, as do many perennials. Well-stocked packet seed displays in larger stores have a good choice of separate colors, but packets of "mixed colors" of the more popular flowers are much in evidence. The best way to use seeds or plants in mixed colors is in drifts between solid-color background and edging flowers. "Cutting rows" of mixed color annuals in the vegetable garden, or small beds planted to mixed colors, are perfectly acceptable. Flower arrangers like mixed-color beds for variety.

Texture. Only experience will show you how to coordinate textures in plants. Certain flowers have coarse, hairy leaves—zinnias, for instance. Planted next to delicate baby's breath, zinnias have a raffish look—better pair them with marigolds or annual gaillardias. Likewise, the dashing green-bronze leaves of cannas overwhelm almost any flower placed near them. This is why landscapers of city parks tame cannas with robust fountain grass or the fiery red salvias.

It is also possible to achieve a filigree effect with proper attention to texture. An edging of cup flower or nierembergia a bedding of love-in-a-mist, and a background of cosmos, for instance, will do it. Plants can be used to hide the defects of others; for instance, the heavy texture of flowers such as medium-height marigolds can be used to hide the legginess of erect plants such as lilies.

AIDS TO PLANNING

It isn't necessary to study numerous books before establishing your first flower bed, but do gather a few publications to help you visualize gardens and compare the merits of various flowers. Send for seed, bulb, and nursery catalogs advertised in garden magazines. With very few exceptions, these firms are fair in their dealings. You would be better off by-passing the few with the ads that scream "amazing," "incredible," "once-in-a-lifetime opportunity." The better plantsmen wax enthusiastic about really good plants, but there is a world of difference between their balanced descriptions and those of the horticultural pitchmen.

Visit municipal gardens, arboretums, and show gardens. There is no better way to see which flowers grow well together and to whet your appetite for adventuring with the new and different. Browse among the bedding plants and seed displays at your local nursery. You'll probably find yourself buying some of each—the bedding plants for instant color and the seeds for economy and the fulfillment of a yen to grow your own.

CLASS OR MASS?

One of the tragedies of modern housing developments is that many beginning gardeners substitute mass for class—rushing to plant quick-growing trees and shrubs to "give their home a settled look." The effect is not bad for a few years, but later you see these same people cutting back or removing the overgrown greenery. Their gardens are overrun with the commonplace. It can be depressing to drive through such neighborhoods, because the majority of the trees and shrubs are low-cost, ordinary, not always desirable species.

If you move into a home with an established garden where many of the plants are coarse, weedy, or of the type that generate an untidy mess, get rid of them before you come to tolerate them. Then you can plan a satisfying garden around the remaining material. Many people feel twinges of conscience at cutting down "perfectly good" living trees and shrubs and throwing away surplus bulbs and perennials. But weeding out is a necessary and continuing process in creating and maintaining a garden.

How much better it is to plan a garden from the beginning to include the better and more beautiful plant materials. Purchase small sizes of choice trees and shrubs as your budget allows, filling in meanwhile with annuals, perennials, and bulbs. By far, the greatest investment in your garden is your time and work. Spend them on high-quality plants that will bring you joy as you watch them grow and develop, instead of humdrum material that takes just as much effort.

Big, bold pink peonies bloom at the same time as iris. Their colors go well together.

No grass in the front yard of this beachside home...only flowers; tuberous-rooted begonias in tubs and hanging baskets, marigolds and geraniums.

PLANTING AND CARING FOR A GARDEN 3

If your budget is flexible and if you have little time to put into the garden, you can buy seedlings from a reputable nursery, plant them, and watch them grow. Or, if you have more time and self confidence than money, you can start with seeds. Many gardeners prefer to grow their own seedlings and transplant them into the beds at the proper time.

Starting seeds indoors. Small seeds, particularly those that are slow to sprout, are best started indoors two to three months prior to the usual date of the last killing frost. Earlier starting is inadvisable because young plants need all the light they can get, and in the dead of winter the days are short. Also, some plants may grow overly large before it is safe to transplant them to the garden.

Planting mixtures and containers. Mixtures should be loose, crumbly, and well-drained. "Milled" or "ground" sphagnum moss is excellent—so are the many prepared potting soil mixes. Do not add any fertilizer to mixtures used for sprouting seeds—more about this on page 22.

You can sprout seeds in any shallow container such as a pot, foil cake pan, or the bottom half of a plasticized-paper milk carton. Good drainage is absolutely necessary; perforate the bottoms of plastic or metal containers with good-sized holes to insure fast drainage.

Sprouting seeds. Fill the container nearly to the top with prepared planting mixture, tamp, thoroughly moisten the mix, and scatter the seeds over the surface. Sprinkle a light covering of the mixture over the seeds (barely cover them). Place the container in a small plastic bag and set in a warm spot (it need not be in the sun). The top of an insulated hot water heater, away from the hot air vent, is an ideal spot. After four or five days begin watch-

Fluorescent light unit for starting seeds in flats. Height is adjustable.

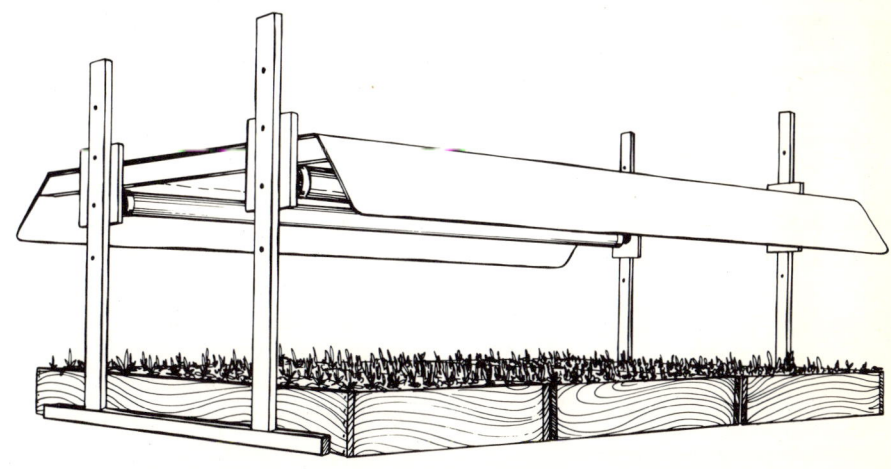

21

ing closely for sprouts; don't become impatient, because as much as two to three weeks may be required for certain slow sprouters. Just as soon as you see signs of life, take the container out of the plastic bag and set it on a sunny window sill or under a fluorescent light (see pages 21 and 23).

Windowsills on the south or west side of the house are best for growing plants because they get the most sun. However, they are too cool to *sprout* seeds. As a general rule, seeds sprout well at 65 to 75 degrees, but young seedlings *grow* best at temperatures of 55 to 60 degrees when the light intensity is low. Read the seed packet carefully and observe special instructions for sprouting or "germinating" the seeds. Certain kinds of seeds—coleus and impatiens, for example—sprout best at soil temperatures of about 80 degrees.

If you live where early spring nights are extremely cold and windows are frosty, move young plants to a warmer area each evening or slide newspaper between them and the cold window glass.

Watering and fertilizing young seedlings. Most gardeners give young seedlings far too much water. A frequent complaint is, "The seeds sprouted, but when the plants started to get some height, they fell over and died." Too much water, too high temperatures, and too little light conspire to create the right conditions for "damping off," a soil-borne disease that attacks and girdles young seedlings at ground level. There are no really effective fungicides for controlling damping off once it has begun; it is best to start anew. The problem can be eliminated by starting off with a topping of sphagnum moss over the chosen planting mixture.

Experiment with "hefting" plant containers to determine if they need water. Pick them up when dry to get the "feel" of their weight; later, if they are heavy, don't add water. Plants use virtually no water when quite small; most of the water loss from containers is due to surface evaporation. When plants grow larger and the days lengthen, however, you have to add water every three or four days.

After plants have grown four to six leaves you may add a very weak solution of "complete" fertilizer (see Chapter 5) to the water every two weeks. Seedlings especially need phosphorous to develop a strong frame and a good root system.

Healthy, "thrifty" seedling, short and stocky.

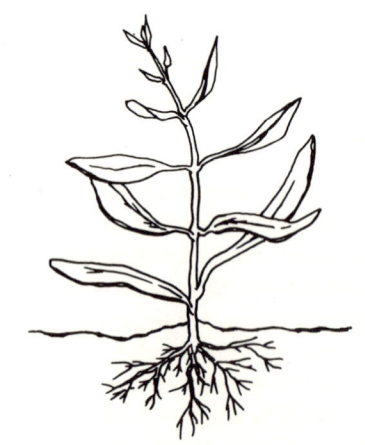
Tall, spindly seedling, grown with too little light.

Seedling girdled and killed by "damping off" disease.

Preparing a seed tray for quick sprouting. Punch drainage holes, fill with fast-draining soil mix, plant seeds and enclose in a plastic bag.

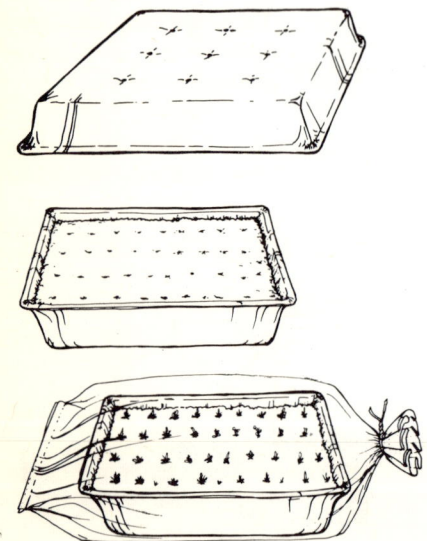

It is important to "leach" containers of good-sized seedlings once every two or three weeks by watering them heavily. This removes the salts that accumulate from the residues of chemical fertilizers and from those left by evaporating water.

Fluorescent lights. I have found that a small, inexpensive, reflector-type fluorescent fixture with two twenty-watt tubes is a good unit for beginners. Ordinary daylight white tubes do a good job of growing plants. There are special tubes on the market that transmit more of the red spectrum to plants; these are especially good for inducing blooms on plants and bringing out the natural flower colors. The best results in sprouting seeds are obtained from lights that can be lowered to a height of only two to three inches from the tops of the seed flats or pots. (Lightweight chains hung from the ceiling are a typical arrangement for adjusting the height.) The radiant energy from fluorescent tubes gently warms the soil and causes seeds to sprout rapidly. You can leave the lights on for twenty-four hours a day for sprouting seeds, or time them for the hours you are awake; either method works well. Seedlings and cuttings grown under lights are tender and succulent; they need special preparation before they are moved out of doors. (See "hardening off" on page 24.) once the started plants are outdoors you can use the fluorescent light for houseplants.

Transplanting indoors. Seedlings can't remain for a prolonged period in the cramped container used for starting them. Prepare a moist, well-drained soil mixture and fill pots of clay, plastic, or peat with the mix, or transplant seedlings into a flat of soil. Use a pencil to punch planting holes to receive the seedlings. "Prick out" the seedlings by gently uprooting them with the pencil point. If the seedlings are quite small, move them in clumps of two or three plants; these can be separated when you transplant to the garden. Set the seedlings in the pots or flats, firm the soil around the roots, and water them lightly. Use no fertilizer in the mix or in the water for a week or ten days following transplanting. Moving the plants shocks them; fertilizer would only add insult to injury because the injured roots cannot take up the amount of nutrients released by chemical fertilizers.

STARTING CUTTINGS INDOORS

Starting new plants from pieces of another plant is called "vegetative reproduction." Almost any plant with fleshy, solid stems or leaves can be reproduced "true-to-type" by rooting a leaf or stem.

Rooting mixtures. Make up a fast-draining rooting mixture such as 50 percent moist peat moss and 50 percent "Sponge-Rok" or "Perlite," or "Terra-Lite" (coarse grade). Do not add fertilizer. Pots of five to six inches in diameter make good containers for rooting; fill them to within one inch of the rim and settle the mix by shaking the pot or tamping the mixture.

"Leaf cuttings." Mature leaves from fleshy plants such as begonias should be taken with stems attached. Do not attempt to save a plant that looks "sick" by rooting a leaf from it; chances are the leaf won't root. Lay the leaves flat on the surface of the soil, embedding the leaf stems to bring the undersurface of the leaf into contact with the soil. It sometimes helps to pin the leaves down with hairpins. Water the container, let it drain, and enclose it in a plastic bag. Set it in a shaded area for a week or so, then move it to a windowsill or under fluorescent lights. (Strong sunlight can overheat cuttings or cause them to sunburn.) Remove the plastic cover after roots have formed, and feed plants lightly with liquid fertilizer every two weeks.

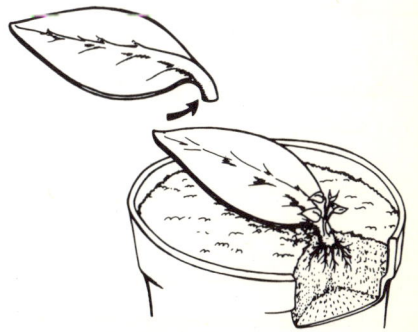

Make leaf cuttings with the stem attached. Cross-section shows how leaf cuttings take root and form new plants.

Stem cutting or "slips." Succulent plants—coleus, impatiens, fibrous-rooted begonias, delphiniums, chrysanthemums, and geraniums*—can be rooted from "slips" or stem cuttings. Use three- to six-inch pieces from the tips of branches. Include two or three joints on each cutting. (You can recognize a joint, or "node," because leaves or branches grow out of it.) Trim off all but the small leaves at the top of the cutting. Make deep holes with a pencil and insert the cuttings until only the leaves protrude above the surface. Then treat as described above for rooting leaves.

Early in the rooting process you

*Allow cuttings of geraniums to dry out for two to three days before planting. This will not harm them and will reduce the possibility of loss due to rotting.

Make stem cuttings from the tips of growing branches, but not those which are flowering. Trim off all but four to six of the top leaves. Punch a hole in the potting mixture with a pencil. Insert the cutting and firm the soil around it. Roots will form along the part of the stem that is imbedded in the soil.

can pull up cuttings occasionally to check their progress. Watch for a thickening that will form at the cut surface; it is called a "callus." When a callus has formed, roots will follow in a week or so.

The speed and reliability of rooting cuttings can be improved by using the proprietary compounds called "rooting hormones," which stimulate the formation of roots. Simply dip the cut ends of the cuttings into the hormones, following the directions.

TRANSPLANTING TO THE GARDEN

Transplanting can be easy if you understand that the young plants are being shifted to a new environment and can be hurt or shocked in the process (unless they are growing in peat pots). A little extra care on your part can make the transition so easy that the plants won't even slow down in growth. Wait until all danger of frost is past and the soil is in good condition to work.

Hardening off. An essential step in transplanting rooted cuttings or seedlings from the house to the garden is the gradual acclimatization called "hardening off." A few days prior to transplanting to the garden, move the seedling containers in early morning to a sunny spot outdoors, away from the wind. Bring in the plants at night for the first two or three days, then leave them outside if temperatures are expected to remain at 50 degrees or higher.

Always do your transplanting in the early morning or evening to reduce shock from wind or strong sunlight. Follow these steps:

1. Water the plants thoroughly the night before transplanting and allow them to drain.

2. Prepare the bed in the garden by spading, raking, and firming the soil. A light application of fertilizer may be worked in.

3. Prepare holes for the transplants. Make the holes two or three times as large as the root structure of the plant. Fill holes with water and allow it to soak into the soil. Repeat.

4. Take plants out of their container. Separate them before planting; retain as much undisturbed soil around their roots as possible. Do not allow roots to become exposed to sun and wind even for a few minutes.

5. Set in the plants to about the same depth as in their original containers. Pull the loose soil into the hole and firm it level with the surrounding soil.

6. Water each plant. This will provide enough moisture to protect the plant while it is becoming accustomed to its new environment.

7. If you must transplant on a hot or windy day, immediately cover the plants with hoods of newspaper held down with clods. This will shade and provide shelter from drying winds. Remove the hoods in the evening.

8. If cutworms are a problem in your garden, set juice or soup cans (with tops and bottoms removed) over the plants.

9. Water plants daily for the first week, then weekly for two weeks.

Dig holes and fill with water. Let it soak in. Leave as much soil as possible around the roots of plants.
Set in the plants to the same depth as in their original containers. Cover the roots, firm, and water with a gentle flow from the hose or with a sprinkling can.

STARTING SEEDS AND BULBS IN THE GARDEN

Millions of flower seeds fail to come up each gardening season because gardeners neglect one or more of these common-sense precautions:

1. Sow seeds at the recommended dates: nothing is gained by planting seeds too early, and you run the risk of having them rot in cold, wet soil. On the other hand, very late seeding produces plants with a short season of bloom.

2. Plant at the recommended depth. Seeds are, after all, only baby plants and often they don't have the strength to push up through layers of soil. As a rule of thumb, cover seeds to a depth equal to two and a half times their diameter. Do not cover very fine seeds; simply press them into the surface of the soil.

3. Soak the seed bed thoroughly a day or two prior to planting. (If you plant and then try to sprinkle on enough water, you may wash away the seeds.)

4. Firm the soil after planting. This brings moist soil particles into firm contact with the seeds and establishes the capillary flow of water from the lower levels in the soil.

5. Protect seedlings from slugs and snails with poison baits. If it appears that a row of seeds has not sprouted in its due time, look closely; you may find a line of stubs, evidence that the seeds sprouted but were eaten by some pest. Bird damage is usually characterized by seedlings being pulled up roots and all, leaving holes. Lay chicken wire over seedlings to prevent bird damage.

The seedbed. I was fortunate to have as a neighbor for many years a man who was frugal in all matters (except hospitality), and especially with seeds. He never "broadcast," or scattered, seeds; instead, he started a few at a time in what he called "nursery rows." He sowed thinly in the nursery rows and transplanted all but a few seedlings while they were still quite small. There was never a gap in a row or bed because his transplants always took.

If a plant was trampled by children or animals, he simply moved in a replacement from the nursery row. Each seedling was dug up with a shovel and moved with a generous amount of undisturbed soil around the root system.

It took me a number of years to conclude that his methods were more sensible than mine. . . . I belonged to the school of "plant thickly where flowers or vegetables are to remain, and thin out the excess." In the hope that his tried-and-true methods will prove valuable to you, let me describe his nursery beds. He set aside a small sunny corner of his garden near the water supply and tool shed. Each year he would add some builder's sand to keep the soil fast-draining and easy to work. In late summer, after transplanting all seedlings, he would

25

begin accumulating vegetable trimmings and leaves (no weeds or spent flowers) in a pile atop the nursery area. Early the following spring he would turn under the resulting compost. The nursery beds were banked up fairly high for good drainage, then raked flat to a width of about eighteen inches. This gave him enough for two rows on each bed. Before planting seeds he would lay a broad plank down the length of the row and walk on it to firm down the soil so that the capillary flow of water would be established.

My old friend carried his small garden tools and seeds in a little "garden box." Included in its neatly arranged contents were two short pegs and a length of chalk line. He placed pegs at the ends of the nursery row and stretched the stout cord between them to mark a straight row. Then, he "opened the row" to a depth of about one inch with the corner of a hoe. Next, he carefully sifted a few seeds along the row and then sprinkled a little soil on the seeds, just enough to hide them. Finally, he tamped the soil atop the seeds with the back of his hoe to insure firm contact. Within a few days his seeds sprouted; they were usually ready for transplanting within three or four weeks. (He kept track of what was growing where by means of labels made of thin slats from apple crates.)

A variation of the preceding technique is necessary where summers are dry. First, the nursery area must be given a thorough soaking and allowed to dry enough to work. The nursery rows should be opened deeply, to three or four inches, and each nursery row should be short—no more than three or four feet.

Sow seeds thinly and give them a light covering of sand or vermiculite. Tamp to firm the soil. Finally, allow water to trickle into the opened furrow until it is full. Cover the furrow with a wide board until seeds sprout. Sprouting will take place rapidly in the moist furrow where seeds are protected from drying winds. Remove the board as soon as the first sprouts appear; wait until evening to do this.

Newer devices for starting seeds in the spring. A latter-day technique utilizes a sheet of clear plastic tacked across a rectangle of one-by-two lumber. The soil should be moistened and seeds sown as usual, but in shallow furrows. The plastic frame becomes a "greenhouse" to concentrate and conserve heat and to prevent moisture loss. You must watch closely and raise one end of the frame slightly when seeds start to sprout. This ventilation is necessary to prevent disease from forming and spreading under the warm, moist "greenhouse."

Clear plastic sheeting can also be stretched over U-shaped hoops like

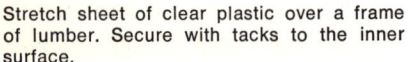
Plastic sheet "cloche" made with inverted "U" frames of heavy wire.

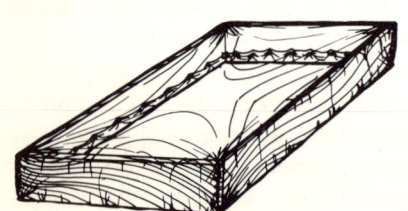
Stretch sheet of clear plastic over a frame of lumber. Secure with tacks to the inner surface.

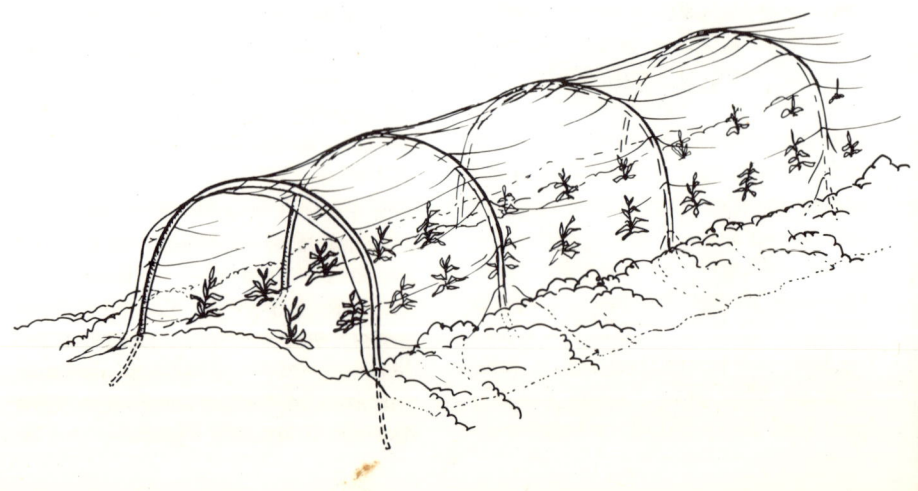

croquet wickets to make a tunnel-like "cloche" over a nursery row. Bury the edges of the plastic securely under the soil to keep gusty spring winds from blowing it away. When days grow warm, raise one edge of the plastic for ventilation. When nights have warmed up, remove the plastic entirely.

Cloches are similar in function to the "coldframes" often found in American gardens. Coldframes are frequently made of window sash hinged on a board frame that has soil mounded up around it to exclude water and to insulate the frame. The back of the frame is higher than the front so that water will drain off the sash. (From the standpoint of safety, clear fiberglass would be preferable to the use of glass.)

WEEDING AND CULTIVATING

Weeding is obviously necessary, not just to maintain your own garden in a respectable condition, but also to reduce the competition between weeds and flowers. I have found that weeding and cultivating go much faster if I pull out and remove the big weeds, including those growing closely around flowering plants. Then, as I hoe out the small weeds in the large open spaces between plants, I accomplish the job of cultivation at the same time. You can make the job of killing weeds much more efficient by working over the hoed area with a rake after an hour or so, when the top layer has dried out. This breaks up the clods and exposes sprouting weed seeds to the drying sun and wind.

The need for weeding and cultivation is greatly decreased by the use of plastic sheeting as a mulch to reduce water loss from evaporation and to prevent weed seedlings from emerging. Some gardeners prefer to use a "natural" mulch of porous materials such as buckwheat, cocoa bean, cottonseed, or peanut hulls.

WATERING OR IRRIGATING

Flowers show unmistakable signs when they need water; they begin to look wilted and later lose color. Plants can recover quickly from minor wilting if given fast treatment. Garden flowers benefit from watering when nature does not provide rain, but it must be deep watering. One of the most common causes of poor growth is shallow penetration of water, particularly in hard soil that tends to crust and bake.

The water hose should not have a nozzle. It is of little use in the garden. Invest in a long, lightweight wand with a "bubbler" on the end to reduce the force of the water. Leave the bubbler in each spot for at least thirty minutes, moving it around while you are busy with other garden chores. I find it handy to scrape up loose soil to make shallow "basins" that impound the water and spread it evenly over the entire bed. Basins or deep irrigation furrows are virtually a necessity in the arid West.

Soaker hoses made of canvas may run the length of a flower bed and be left in place during the dry season. They are less apt to encourage foliage diseases than the perforated plastic hoses that spray water on the foliage. However, plastic hoses may be turned over so that the water jets down into the soil instead of wetting the foliage of plants.

Large perennial plants—and trees and shrubs—can go off in color and can even drop their foliage during prolonged dry spells. This is particularly true of plants in lawn areas or on steep slopes. Soil can become baked so solid that water will begin to run off after only a few minutes of sprinkling. "Root irrigators" can solve this problem. They are hollow, pointed rods connected to the water hose through a grip valve. A jet of water makes deep holes hydraulically and flows water down into the root area. If you "root irrigate" the shaded areas under trees, you will water most of the root system. Occasional root irrigations will soften the soil so that surface-applied water will again soak in.

Weeding and cultivating come invariably with gardening, it is true, but you can do much to minimize their drain on your time and energy. Here are some of the newer labor-saving ideas:

GARDENING IN CONTAINERS

Container gardening is particularly recommended for gardeners with small back yards, for older people,

27

and for gardeners who have little time for cultivating and weeding. The optimum arrangement is to place containers on a patio or on a firm, deep mulch of pebbles or decorative rock that can be sprayed to eliminate weeds. Patio containers should be on castered frames to facilitate moving and cleaning.

For best growth of plants, soil for containers should be exceptionally porous and fast-draining. (Ordinary garden soil tends to dry and shrink away from the sides of the containers.) Mix equal parts of sand or sponge rock, peat moss or composted sawdust, and soil. Mix well to avoid the formation of layers in the containers. Fill the containers to within three inches of the top; the "head space" forms a reservoir to make watering easier.

Containers should be deep, to reduce the frequency of watering. They need not be expensive; you can adapt the glazed tile used for lining chimneys, or you can dress up lengths of large-diameter concrete pipe. Use different lengths for variety. Be sure that heavy containers are set on slightly raised areas of rock or pebbles to promote fast drainage.

A novel and highly effective "container" may be made of a cylinder of chicken wire stuffed with natural or "unmilled" sphagnum moss. The cylinder may be double-walled, with a open center core to decrease its weight. You may hang the cylinder on a length of heavy wire or hold it erect with sturdy stakes. Sphagnum moss holds water well but has virtually no natural fertility, so you will need to include a dilute solution of fertilizer with every watering. Use the cylinder to grow trailing plants such as lobelias, dwarf tomatoes, dwarf impatiens, and trailing types of fuchsias. Moisten the moss, spread it apart, insert the plant's root system, then firm the moss around the roots. Leave a root ball of soil with the plants and they will establish faster.

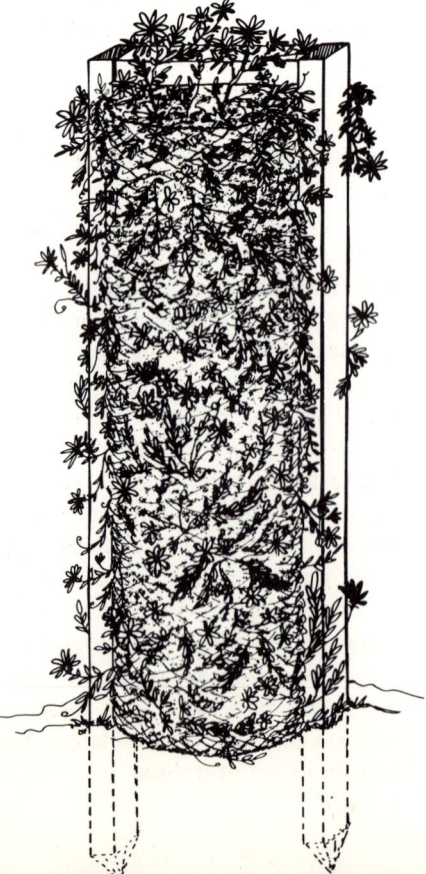

Chicken wire cylinder stuffed with natural sphagnum moss and planted with trailing flowers. By midsummer, there will be a "tower of flowers."

MULCHES

Mulches can do much to decrease water evaporation and the work of weeding and cultivating. Temporary organic mulches have been mentioned previously. "Permanent" mulches are of two general types: chunks or chips of wood or bark, and fragments of decorative rock. The bark is less expensive, but it does have the tendency to float away during heavy rainstorms. Children are less apt to cause damage if they pick up and toss chunks of bark.

There is a trend toward gardening with mulches, particularly rock mulches, even to the extent of replacing areas of lawn with them. When rock mulches are used, gardeners employ "planting wells" of redwood boards, bricks, or of the

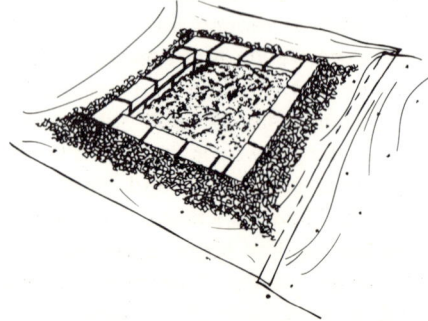

Constructing a "planting well" in stone mulch. Cut out a square of plastic for the well, excavate 12 inches deep, construct the well, and fill with topsoil.

Cross-section of completed well. Surface is elevated for drainage.

handy precast concrete circles. It is easy to water the small areas of soil inside the planting wells and to keep them free of weeds.

Stone mulches tend to absorb and reflect heat. Generally speaking, the heat-loving summer annuals or flowering shrubs respond well to the growing environment created by rock mulches.

Commercial landscapers often lay a sheet of plastic under stone, bark, or wood-chip mulches to keep down weeds. They make small slits at intervals in the sheets to allow water to penetrate. These slits sometimes prove inadequate to handle the drainage from heavy rains; you may need more holes to avoid ponding.

Weed and grass killers are now so efficient that an occasional tour around the garden with a box of granular weed killer or a spray can full of herbicide will keep rock or bark mulches free of weeds. Follow the directions carefully; excessive applications of herbicides can gravitate into planting wells and kill your flowers as well as weeds.

PICKING OFF OR SHEARING FLOWERS

You will see on seed packets and in garden catalogs the admonition to "pick off spent blossoms." This seems like a chore; is it really necessary? No, it is not—and most gardeners don't take the time and trouble to do it regularly. Yet, picking or shearing off blossoms when they are past their prime will keep the plants in bloom for a longer period. Seeds usually begin to form within the blossoms as they mature. The formation of seeds can rob other parts of the plant of nutrients, because reproduction takes priority over the other functions of the plant. Removing spent flowers from little plants such as pansies is rather easy; you can pinch the stems off a bed of pansies in no time flat. You will need pruning shears for heavy-stemmed plants such as tall marigolds and zinnias. Vary the length of stem taken, to keep plants looking neat, not clipped.

WINTER CLEANUP

The kinds of flowers with seed heads that cling to the dried plants can be left over winter for feeding birds. In northern states the frozen tops of perennials may be left in place to provide a protective mulch, and removed during spring cleanup. Across the South and on the West Coast, where winters are relatively mild and rains are frequent, a thorough fall cleanup reduces the possibility of buildup of plant diseases that live over in dead leaves and rubble. Snails, slugs, and bugs also harbor in dead litter; a fall cleanup reduces their numbers.

4 TOOLS AND EQUIPMENT

Tools are extensions of a gardener's hands that allow him to accomplish more. No two people use the same equipment in gardening, nor do they use it in the same way. One can only suggest tools that may prove most useful to you. Purchase them carefully—heft them—see if they fit your hands and if they are well balanced. These simple precautions should minimize the risk of your buying a tool that will end up hanging unused in the tool shed.

HAND TOOLS

The tools listed below are necessary for one to establish and maintain a flower garden:

shovel, preferably long-handled and round-pointed;
hoe, with either square or triangular blade;
spading fork, four-tined, long-handled;
rake, sharp-tined, lightweight;
cultivator-weeder, claw-type, long or short-handled;
pick-axe, if soil is hard in the summer;
trowel, with forged steel blade and sturdy, forged shank;
pruning shears, one pair pocket-size, the other long-handled;
sharpening file or stone;
ball of strong twine or "chalk line" and stakes to mark straight rows.

In any case, don't waste your money on cheap tools. Handles snap, blades crack, tines bend or break, steel blades won't hold an edge, trowels bend double, etc. Good hand tools should last for ten years or more. If you are small or slight of build, buy the special sizes of hand tools developed for women. Actually, some burly men also prefer these junior-sized hand tools because they can get them into smaller corners.

POWER TOOLS

In small gardens power tools are not necessary, but they do make certain jobs go faster. In large gardens power tillers, edgers, trimmers, compost shredders, and sprayers can be a big help where frequency of use can justify the investment. They also come in handy for gardeners who must curtail physical activity for reasons of health.

QUICK CHECKLIST

Sooner or later you will need the following: wheelbarrow or garden cart (except for very small gardens); bench for potting (make it high for comfort in working); wooden flats, peat pots, and clay pots of assorted sizes and in a range of depths and diameters; hardware-cloth sieve for screening soil mixes; garbage cans or wooden boxes filled with sand, peat moss, or composted sawdust; one- to three-gallon tank sprayer; garden hose and sprinkler; low-pressure spreader nozzle or bubbler for hose; hose-end applicator for foliar feeding (explained on page 35); assorted labels (of wood, heavy foil, or plastic); fertilizer, high analysis, complete (see Chapter 5); fungicide for disinfecting seeds and bulbs; insecticide, a mixture to kill both sucking and chewing types.

Of course, most gardeners will

also need a lawn mower, a flexible-tined lawn and leaf rake, etc., but these are not within the province of a book on flower gardening.

MAINTENANCE

Most gardeners begin by storing tools and equipment in their garages, but this arrangement has disadvantages unless a section can be partitioned off for this special purpose. Much to be preferred is a small shed, which can eliminate the annoyance of grass clippings and garden soil that are carried into the garage on tools and equipment.

Sheds also have the feature of extra safety, because the gasoline used for engines may be stored away from the house.

Tool sheds can be built to be decorative, or landscaped to be unobtrusive. Tool sheds should have fairly high walls on which long-handled tools may be hung. A concrete floor with a sill, raised for drainage, reduces the dampness in a shed and eliminates the menace of rust. A wide door and a ramp for easy handling of wheeled power equipment should be provided. A generous overhang prevents rain from driving in around the door.

Store the manuals for care of power tools and equipment in a plastic bag and hang it in a cupboard. Refer to the manuals occasionally to maintain a preventive maintenance program. Also, store a can of linseed oil with your tools and apply it to wooden handles twice yearly to reduce drying and cracking.

To prolong the life of tools, scrape off heavy deposits of garden soil after each use. Wash off minor soil deposits with hot water, which heats the metal parts and causes them to dry quickly, thus reducing rust damage. A light coating of oil should be applied to metal parts of tools prior to winter storage.

5 IMPROVING AND MANAGING YOUR SOIL

Until now you may have given little thought to soil, except when you have had to wash it out of clothes, clean it off shoes, or move it in a wheelbarrow. Yet soil is the key element in gardening, even more than plants or planning.

Is there a single factor that distinguishes a "green-thumb" gardener from one who is not particularly successful? In all probability, the difference lies in the good gardener's appreciation of soil as *living matter* that must be kept healthy in order to do its part in producing plant growth.

This book discusses soil amendments and fertilizers before touching on soils and soil management because not many soils can grow plants well without a few improvements on Nature.

SOIL AMENDMENTS

The ideal soil for most plants is loose, well-aerated, and easy to cultivate. Old-timers describe it as "mellow." Water soaks into mellow soil readily, and the soil does not bake hard during the summer. The ideal soil is deep, well drained, and fertile. The ideal soil is usually *not* a natural product; it is developed through a program of soil improvement based on soil amendments.

Soil amendments contain little or no major nutrients and are added primarily to improve the structure or water retention of the soil, or to change its pH (degree of acidity or alkalinity, which is sometimes referred to as "sweetness"). pH is discussed in detail on page 37.

Soil amendments are sold in great volume to home gardeners and professional landscapers. Peat moss can be bought by the bag or bale, sawdust can be ordered from many lumber yards, manure can be purchased from stables or feedlots; cotton, peanuts, or rice hulls can be obtained in the South or West. All these and many others serve the same purposes: they loosen heavy or dense soil; they increase the water and nutrient-holding capacity of light or loose soils. Such amendments also make the soil easier to work and they promote better root development.

Soil amendments are not permanent; they must be renewed every two or three years. As they decay they release varying amounts of plant foods, but by no means should amendments be considered as replacements for fertilizers.

Sawdust and manure. Sawdust is the most economical soil amendment and is used in vast quantities by commercial horticulturists. Fresh manure is losing favor because it usually has a high content of weed seeds. It also may be difficult to obtain except in rural areas. Steamed or processed manures are practically free of weed seeds and are available at garden supply stores.

Lime and gypsum. Chemicals used for making soil more acid or more alkaline are also called amendments. They are not fertilizers, because plants take little of the chemicals into their tissues. Lime and gypsum are soil amendments, not fertilizers.

Lime is used on acid or "sour" soils to neutralize or lessen the degree of acidity. When soils are made less acid, the nutrients in them, notably iron and phosphorous, become more available to plants. As limestone breaks down it releases calcium or magnesium, which provides a secondary benefit in areas where excessive soil moisture has washed away the calcium or magnesium compounds needed to prevent acids from developing in the soil.

Gypsum is especially valuable on alkaline soils, where it neutralizes excess salts and granulates the soil. These chemical reactions are accomplished without making the soil more basic. Gypsum also has a temporary granulating effect upon heavy clay, but organic amendments do a better job of making the soil more mellow.

FERTILIZERS

Fertilizers may be either "mineral" (sometimes called "chemical"), "organic," or a mixture of both. They are called "balanced" or "complete" fertilizers if they contain approximately equal quantities of the three major plant foods—nitrogen, phosphorus, and potassium, or "potash."

Dry or granular fertilizers. Wise shoppers are guided by the analysis label when buying dry or granular fertilizers. The label is required by law to list the units or percentages by weight of the major plant foods. Add up the units of the three major plant foods on the label and compare prices between brands. The chemical symbols of the nutrients are used; nitrogen is listed as N, phosphorus as P_2O_5, and potassium as K_2O. Keeping in mind that nitrogen is the most expensive of the three major components, you should be able to decide which brand is the best buy. Ordinary complete fertilizers have between twenty and twenty-five pounds (units) of plant food per hundred pounds of fertilizer. Everything else in the container is inert carrier or filler. Carriers are a necessary part of the chemical compounds that are used in fertilizers.

Certain brands of fertilizer are more expensive because they include natural organic materials such as tankage, cottonseed meal, or other vegetable byproducts. You must decide whether the slow-release value of this organic matter is worth the additional cost. (This prolonged release is attained through the slow decomposition of the organic matter and the subsequent release of nutrients in forms available to plants.)

There are also some newer granular fertilizers—light-weight, high-analysis products, containing as many as thirty to forty-five units of plant food per hundred pounds. They are expensive per bag but are often more economical per unit of plant food. Some have the added advantage of slow release of the plant foods, which reduces the danger of injury to plants through burning. Their nitrogen content may be composed of urea-formaldehyde, an excellent, long-lasting material that is safe to use around most plants. Although slow-release fertilizers are relatively safe to use, it is possible to burn or kill plants or lawns by applying more than the recommended amount.

Nitrogen can be purchased separately as nitrate of soda (a commonly used and inexpensive form), ammonium nitrate, ammonium sulphate, urea, or urea-formaldehyde. Nitrogen in any form is a good lawn food but is not adequate when used alone for flowers because it stimulates vegetative growth at the expense of blossoms. Stick to balanced fertilizers for flowers. Flowers need phosphorus and potassium for strong stems and healthy blossoms, unless a soil test (see page 37) indicates otherwise.

On the left, medium-analysis, bulky granular fertilizer. Usually dissolves incompletely. On the right, high-analysis, granular, soluble fertilizer. Dissolves completely; applied with hose-end sprayer or sprinkling can.

'Knee-Hi' mixed colors sweet peas.
Courtesy Ferry-Morse Seed Co.

Gloriosa Daisy. *Courtesy Ferry-Morse Seed Co.*

Three hybrid petunias—'White Cascade,' 'Pink Cascade,' and 'Sugar Daddy'—with 'Redstone Rocket' snapdragons in rear.
Courtesy Pan-American Seed Co.

Liquid or soluble fertilizers. These are very popular for flower gardening. While much more expensive per unit of plant food, they are handy, clean, fast-acting, and usually less wasteful. They should be diluted strictly according to directions to avoid burning plants.

Soluble mineral fertilizers usually come in one- to ten-pound containers for garden use (smaller sizes for house plants). Soluble fertilizers dissolve quickly in water and can be poured around the roots of flowers or sprayed on the foliage. You must be very careful not to make the solutions too strong, particularly when foliar-feeding. Either foliar- or root-feeding is good, but foliar-feeding works best on sandy soil where fertilizers tend to leach away in surplus water. Foliar-feeding is most effective during daytime hours when the stomata (minute openings in the surfaces of leaves) are fully open.

Liquid natural or organic fertilizers are usually fish byproducts, often fortified with soluble chemical fertilizers. They act slowly as compared to the soluble mineral fertilizers, but contain minor nutrients and protein breakdown compounds (such as amino acids) not present in mineral products. Liquid organic fertilizers work best when foliar-fed during warm weather. Nothing can match them for putting extra "finish" on flowers.

Fertilizer tablets. A number of formulas are available in tablets, which are of three major types:

1. Soluble tablets that dissolve in water. These are popular for house plants because they are convenient and clean. Nutrients from this type of tablet last only one to three weeks in the soil, necessitating frequent applications. Pot plants that are fertilized with tablets should be set in the sink and watered heavily once each month. This "leaching" washes away fertilizer residues that could otherwise burn plants.

2. Surface-applied tablets made from urea-formaldehyde nitrogen plus slow-release phosphorus and potash. These are relatively safe to use, and one application can feed container plants for four to six months. The gradual, uniform release of nutrients promotes plant health and sustains blossoming.

3. Root-zone tablets made from densely compressed urea-formaldehyde nitrogen plus slow-release phosphorus and potash. These last for one to two years and are particularly good for new plantings of trees, shrubs, and roses. These tablets will not burn roots. Soil bacteria break down the urea-formaldehyde nitrogen to an absorbable form.

Controlled-release fertilizers. The newest of the granular fertilizers feature a gradual, metered release of nutrients that feeds plants over an extended period. Some of these have rather large granules that dissolve slowly in soil water; others have synthetic coatings that let nutrients leak out slowly. Because of their relatively high cost, these fertilizers are used mainly in potting mixtures, house plants, patio plants, and roses. Gardeners who have learned how to use these sophisticated materials are experiencing excellent results, both when controlled-release fertilizers are used alone and when they are used in conjunction with liquid feeding.

"Odds and ends" fertilizers. Depending on locality, one may or may not encounter recommendations for bonemeal, hoof and hornmeal, tankage, bloodmeal, cottonseed meal, etc. Gardeners with strong ties to tradition swear by these old fertilizers because they know how to use them and, unquestionably, they get good results. These fertilizers date back to the days when synthetic slow-release fertilizers and foliar-feeding were unknown. All of them release plant nutrients slowly and evenly, but are comparatively expensive when measured by the units

On the left, high-analysis, liquid, soluble fertilizer. Dissolves completely for spraying on or pouring around plants, but tends to settle unless shaken frequently. On the right, fertilizer tablets. Large ones are for root-zone application, smaller sizes for surface application on various sizes of containers for plants.

of plant nutrients they contain. Unfortunately, they also have a tendency to create odors and to encourage the breeding of gnats and flies.

Poultry manure deserves special mention. It has a high content of nutrients, so much that it burns plants if not first composted with peat moss, wood shavings, sawdust, or similar material. Composting also renders it somewhat less aromatic. Poultry manure contains a relatively high percentage of nitrogen and has a remarkable ability to make flowers grow.

RECOMMENDATIONS FOR FEEDING

Flower beds. Make it a practice to dig in about two pounds of balanced granular fertilizer per 100 square feet when you are spading flower beds. Turn it under as you spade, and mix the fertilizer with the soil down to the eight-inch level. Don't prepare the bed and then scatter the fertilizer on top. Certain nutrients such as phosphorus tend to remain where you put them in the soil and will not work their way down into the root zone.

Bulbs. Spring bulbs need little more fertilizer than an initial application. Summer bulbs such as dahlias, cannas, and caladiums benefit from foliar-feeding, root-zone tablets, or controlled-release granular fertilizers.

Annuals and perennials. Annuals and perennials can be given a "starter solution" at transplanting and can be foliar-fed once or twice during the season or stimulated with a solution of soluble fertilizer poured around the roots. Watch the color and condition of plants. If they begin to turn yellow, slow down in growth, or go out of bloom, give them a light application of fertilizer. The new controlled-release fertilizers, worked into the soil at 1 lb. per 10 sq. ft., will feed annuals for an entire growing season.

Container-grown plants. Container-grown plants need more frequent applications of fertilizer than garden plants because of their restricted root-feeding areas. A feeding of soluble fertilizer each two to three weeks should be sufficient. Plants respond dramatically to foliar-feeding if they have begun to lose color or foliage due to starvation.

Urea-formaldehyde-based container tablets will supply all the major nutrients needed by container plants for four to six months. Certain formulations of granular controlled-release fertilizers are engineered to feed plants fully for nine months or longer with a single application.

MICRONUTRIENTS

Such "minor" elements as copper, zinc, iron, manganese, molybdenum, and boron are occasionally in short supply in soils, particularly those that are very sandy, alkaline, or acid. Most micronutrients are needed in such minute quantities by plants that only a "trace" is required, explaining the common name of "trace elements" that is sometimes used to designate micronutrients.

You can buy these preparations in nearly all good garden stores, but check with your local county agent before investing in micronutrients. Follow the directions carefully, especially with the soluble preparations that are sprayed on the foliage. Even a slight excess of certain micronutrients can cause the foliage to be disfigured.

Garden plants in the West and Southwest often show little or no response to standard fertilizers because certain key nutrients and micronutrients are made unavailable to plants by the action of alkali. Try making the soil more acid by adding powdered sulphur; ask your County Agent for the recommended rates of application. Plants in Florida often show only a limited response to standard fertilizers because the sandy Florida soils are almost devoid of micronutrients.

TYPES OF SOILS

Once one understands that most soils need improvement, one can consider the various types of soil that make up one's own good—or not so good—earth.

LIVING SOILS

Bake a pan of soil in an oven for two hours at 500 degrees and it is made sterile. But if you set the sterilized soil in the open air for a few weeks and add water occasionally, life will return. Microorganisms—good, bad, and indifferent—blow in on dust or flow in with supposedly pure tap water.

Healthy garden soil literally teems with molds, fungi, and bacteria. Hold a handful to your nose and breathe in the warm, fecund smell. What you are smelling is largely the natural and necessary breakdown of organic matter—leaves, roots, peat moss, etc.—and mineral particles.

To comprehend the magnitude of the work done by microorganisms, consider that the earth was once an orb of solid, bare rock and bodies of water. Raging streams fed by torrential rains cut, gouged, and pulverized the rock into gravel, sand, and silt, yet it remained rock until life was created. Organisms then went to work in the moist soil, digesting tiny rock fragments and using them to build their own living tissue. Multiplying at fantastic rates, living in part on the decaying tissues of their antecedents, these microorganisms in turn fed more complex life—simple plants and rudimentary animals. Eons of life produced larger and more involved plants and animals. But in the formation of soil their *death* was more important than their life. Their decay created the thin mantle of topsoil that, warmed by the sun, supports all life.

Decay of animal and vegetable matter releases the mineral nutrients locked in tissues. The released and thereby "available" nutrients are in a form that can be easily absorbed by plant roots. Decay also creates complicated and little-understood byproducts that stimulate plants.

Your challenge as a gardener is to maintain a high level of microbiological activity in the soil by regularly adding organic matter and nutrients in the form of fertilizers.

"BITS-AND-PIECES" SOIL

A soil scientist can take a shovel, a set of sieves or screens, and a magnifying glass into a meadow or forest and, after a few minutes of digging, tell you how the soil was formed. He can look at the shape and size of *bits and pieces* of soil and surmise whether wind, waves, gravity, or volcanic action deposited them, or whether the soil resulted from in-place deterioration of rock by freezing, thawing, and plant activity.

Such a clean-cut analysis would be difficult around many homes, where excavating and filling has disturbed or replaced the soil Nature laid down. Your garden soil might vary from solid clay in one area to loose, fertile loam in another.

ACID OR ALKALINE SOILS

Some time ago a simple scale called pH was devised to indicate the acidity of soils. The scale runs from 1 to 14. The middle, pH 7, is the point at which soil is neither acid ("sour") nor alkaline ("sweet"), but neutral. Numbers below pH 7 indicate acid soil—numbers above 7 indicate alkaline soil.

The easiest way to understand how the pH scale applies to soil is to interpret it thusly:

pH Reading

Below pH 4.3—Extremely acid
pH 4.3 to 4.9—Strongly acid
pH 5 to 6.5 —Moderately to slightly acid
pH 6.6 to 7.3—Neutral, for all practical purposes
pH 7.4 to 8 —Alkaline
above pH 8 —Very alkaline

Most flowers, trees, and shrubs grow best when the soil pH tests 6.5 to 7.

Inexpensive kits may be purchased if you wish to test your own soil for pH. Your County Agent or Farm Advisor can tell you how to take a soil sample for more thorough testing by a county or state agency or by a private laboratory. It is entirely possible that he will tell you not to bother about testing the pH of your soil if you live in an area where most soils are neutral or nearly so. He can advise you on the kind and quantity of soil amendments needed to correct acid or alkaline conditions if applications are indicated by tests.

ORGANIC SOILS

These rich-looking soils contain a high proportion of highly decayed organic matter called "humus," occasionally in combination with sand. Humus is characterized by very fine particles. It has a high degree of electrochemical activity that enables it to absorb and store large quantities of fertilizer. Most humus soils are found on drained swamps or peat bogs. Some humus soils are brown, fibrous, and acid in pH reaction; others are black or grayish and often basic (alkaline) in reaction. Never buy "black dirt" without finding first its pH; you may discover that such soil can do more harm than good.

Organic soils are relatively easy to cultivate and weed. Seeds sprout quickly, and newly transplanted seedlings root readily. Water soaks in rapidly except after a prolonged drought.

Organic soils have two major peculiarities: they tend to dry up and blow away, and they occasionally may require applications of micronutrients to give plants a balanced diet. Mixing heavier soils with organic soils reduces their tendency to blow. Mixing should be thorough to prevent the formation of dense layers that impede the passage of water and roots.

CLAY SOILS

If a garden soil contains enough clay to make it sticky when wet and to cause it to bake hard when dry, it is called a clay soil. Clay particles are very tiny; they pack together to make a dense, plastic soil. While clay is occasionally found in almost pure form, it is most often encountered in combination with varying amounts of sand, silt, or gravel.

Clay soils are blessed with a high water-holding capacity and often with high natural fertility. With proper attention, they can be made into responsive, rewarding soils. Clay warms up slowly in the spring and requires several days after a rain to dry out enough to be worked. The "adobe" clay of the West holds water so stubbornly that farmers work it during dry, summer months, using heavy machinery to crush the clods.

Improving clay soils requires large quantities of soil amendments and, if desired, sand. The job can be strenuous because of the volume of amendments that must be hauled in and thoroughly mixed with the soil. You can make the job easier by improving a small part of your garden at a time and by working the clay only when it is slightly moist but not wet.

The least expensive organic amendment for loosening clay soils is sawdust. Before spreading sawdust, pulverize the soil by spading or tilling. Next, apply a three- to four-inch layer of sawdust and mix it in thoroughly. Hardwood or softwood sawdust works equally well. When using sawdust scatter two to five pounds of nitrogen fertilizer evenly over a hundred square feet of garden area in order to counteract the tendency of fresh sawdust to cause nitrogen starvation in plants. Mix in the nitrogen fertilizer as you spade. If you neglect adding nitrogen, plants in the sawdust-soil mixture will turn yellow because soil bacteria will work overtime to break down the sawdust and will rob nitrogen from plant roots during the process. Sawdust rots and eventually disappears; dig in an additional one or two inches every two or three years.

Mixing sand with clay. Sand alone is not adequate for loosening clay. The mixture will continue to bake hard during hot, dry spells. However, sand and sawdust mixed with clay can create a very desirable soil consistency. Use about one part sand to three parts sawdust by volume.

Mixing peat moss or compost with clay. Peat moss or redwood compost is excellent for loosening and aerating clay. These products are more expensive than sawdust, but are also longer lasting and more convenient. Many other desirable amendments, mostly tree bark products, are available. Don't overlook leaves and garden waste as a means of improving clay. They can be thrown together in a pile and composted (see Glossary).

SILTY SOILS

Silt is composed of particles intermediate in size between clay and sand. The particles are all about the same size and shape and tend to pack together. This makes a hard, gritty soil that is slow to absorb water and quick to dry out. Silt has little natural fertility but can be improved more easily than clay. Organic amendments loosen silty soils and promote water penetration.

Hardpans. "Hardpans" are often found in association with silty soils. Before going about improving the topsoil, dig a test hole about two feet deep. If you encounter a very hard layer (often stained or rusty in color), pulverize it under all flowerbeds, and mix in organic amendments to keep it from sealing into an impervious barrier. Hardpans restrict the vertical movement of water in soil, which causes poor drainage and a tendency to dry out quickly. Breaking up hardpans under a number of flower beds can be hard work; you may elect to build up raised beds to get drainage.

SANDY SOILS

Sandy soils contain particles of sand of varying size and shape as their principal ingredient. They may also contain clay, silt, gravel, and organic fractions. Sand has little or no electrochemical activity, thus possesses little ability to absorb and store plant foods.

Sandy soils require special gardening techniques. Everything applied to sand—fertilizer, peat moss, clay, compost, water—soon gravitates to lower levels where it is lost to plants. There is no escaping the necessity of frequent additions of nutrients and amendments to sand; neglect the feeding of plants every month or so and they stop growing. Neglect adding organic matter regularly and sand loses its ability to store water in reserve for plants. Micronutrient deficiencies often show up in plants grown on sand. These deficiencies may cause distinct color changes in leaves, such as loss of chlorophyll or bronzing or purpling.

Once gardeners get the feel of working with sand, they like it. Sand warms up fast in the spring, allowing earlier planting and faster maturing of plants than on clay soils. Sandy soils can often be worked immediately following a rain, without fear of soil compaction. Weeding is a breeze, seeds sprout easily, cuttings root dependably, and the soil never bakes or crusts. There is always the problem of grit being tracked and blown into the house, but this diminishes as lawns and groundcovers take hold.

LOAMY SOILS

Fortunate is the gardener with loamy soil. Loam is formed of a mixture of sand, silt, clay, and organic matter. It can vary from very loose "sandy loam" to rather heavy "clay loam." In virgin loam (not previously gardened) organic matter is often high.

The management of loam is mostly a matter of maintaining or increasing its content of organic matter and avoiding compacting it when it is wet. Loam is easy to cultivate and needs only moderate amounts of fertilizer to produce good plant growth.

UNUSUAL SOILS

Scattered about the country are patches of odd soils such as caliche, marl, gravel, shale, and "rock flour" (decomposed granite, etc.). These soils have little desirable topsoil, and it is often lost or displaced in grading or leveling. All have a limited natural fertility. Unless gardeners in these areas can afford to excavate flower beds to a depth of one foot and fill with good topsoil, they had best restrict their gardening to containers, where adequate levels of water and fertility can be easily maintained. In preparing soil for containers, mix equal parts of sand, peat moss, and sawdust or shavings. Mix in three to four pounds of high-nitrogen fertilizer per cubic yard. Moisten the soil pile and let it stand for two weeks before using.

LAYERS OF SOIL

If you were to dig a deep hole in your yard, you might be amazed at the layers showing up at various levels. Many soils are underlaid with gravel or sand. Others have a tough, dense layer, like soft rock, just below spade depth—the hardpan referred to earlier. Loam frequently grades into solid rock.

Plants are affected by more than the topsoil—the "icing" on the layer cake. Even dainty flowers send roots one to two feet deep. Some garden flowers can push a heavy root ten feet deep. Plants need the underlying layers of soil—the subsoil—as a reservoir of water and nutrients to carry them through the periods between feedings and waterings. Larger plants send roots deep into the subsoil as anchors against the wind.

Any obstacle to root penetration forces plants to concentrate roots in the shallow topsoil layer. Hardpan is the most common obstacle; you may have to break it up with a pick-axe every few years and incorporate organic amendments.

There is little that the average gardener can do to change his subsoil. If it has a high water table much of the year, he can lay drainage tile. If it is very alkaline, he can install drainage tile to increase the efficiency of leaching by flooding. If the topsoil is shallow and rests on rocky subsoil, he can build up beds, which is usually cheaper than excavating.

CAPILLARITY

The air spaces between soil particles interconnect and serve as thousands of soda straws to suck up moisture from lower levels. Capillarity supplies the "suction." Evaporation at the soil's surface actually pulls moisture up from below. This helps to maintain water reserves that would otherwise be lost by drainage to lower soil levels. Capillarity is the reason soil can stay moist for days after a heavy rain.

CALL ON THE EXPERTS

If you continue to have soil problems, request the assistance of the agricultural department of your state university or see your County Agent or Farm Advisor. Even urban counties employ these experts to assist gardeners. Their advice is free. They are listed under "County Offices" in the phone book. Look for "Cooperative Extension Service" or "Agricultural Extension Service."

CONTROLLING NATURAL ENEMIES 6

Killing living things—even "bugs," snails, and caterpillars—disturbs some gardeners. All gardeners have an innate love and respect for Nature; some hate to upset what they believe to be Nature's plan for life around them. Every vestige of civilization disturbs the balance of Nature; therefore, it is impossible for a "civilized" flower garden to coexist with insects and diseases. One or the other must dominate. Thus, most gardeners use insecticides and fungicides to maintain protected islands of plants in the midst of a hostile environment. They use pest controls because they must, *only* when they must.

Pest control is not a particularly enjoyable facet of gardening because it is essentially destructive. Thus, beginning gardeners are often tempted to try the ignore-the-pest-problem-and-maybe-it-will-go-away system. They delay spraying or dusting until much later than is advisable.

The pest situation must be dealt with intelligently. Seek the advice of a knowledgeable local nurseryman, and get as much literature as you can from your state university's agricultural college and manufacturers. You will soon discover that most garden problems are not caused by exotic insects or obscure maladies, but by one or more of the easily recognized and controllable pests.

INSECTS

Not all insects are harmful to plants; most are beneficial: wasps, bees, ladybugs, praying mantids and lacewing flies, for instance, feed on harmful insects. For this reason you should spray or dust only plants that show signs of insect buildup. Regular dousings of home grounds with insecticides as a preventive measure are usually self-defeating. Beneficial predators are killed along with pests, and generations of harmful insects may build up a genetic resistance that enables a few tough specimens to survive and, in turn, reinfest your garden.

"Chewing" and "sucking" insects. Some gardeners succeed without learning any more than the rudiments of insect identification and control. Their secret is their ability to classify insects by the damage they cause. "Chewing insects" are equipped with strong mouth parts to devour all or parts of stems, buds, leaves, blossoms, roots, fruit, etc. The characteristic damage leaves little doubt that a chewing insect is involved.

"Sucking insects" (the true "bugs") such as aphids have needle-like beaks that puncture plant tissues. They suck the juices of plants, usually leaving tiny spots or curled and disfigured leaves.

Watch for aphids (plant lice) on tender growing tips.

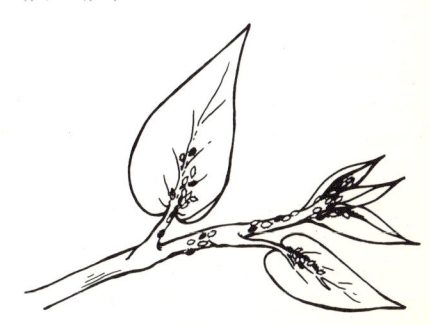

Thrips. "Thrips," very tiny sucking insects, feed inside flower buds and cause distorted, often lopsided flower buds or, in extreme cases, a complete blighting of blossoms.

Mites. Mites, or "red spider mites," bring about damage somewhat similar to that caused by sucking insects, except that they often leave a dusty, webby residue on the undersides of leaves. (Technically, mites are not insects, but are more closely related to spiders.)

What if one can't find the cause of the damage? A little sleuthing may narrow the field. If small, granular deposits of excreta or "frass" are found on leaves or on the ground below the plant, a borer or a chewing insect is probably the source. If you find holes the size of peas or beans cut in the leaves, but little or no excreta, earwigs may be involved. If large, irregular pieces of leaves or entire leaves disappear overnight, the trouble is probably slugs or snails.

Slugs, snails, and earwigs. Slugs, snails, and earwigs operate mostly at night; shine a flashlight on leaves, and you can sometimes catch them at work. Earwigs and certain night-feeding beetles drop off if plants are shaken.

Cutworms. Cutworms, fat, voracious larvae, frequently attack newly transplanted seedlings, girdling or cutting them at soil level; they, too, operate at night. (They may be foiled by fitting young plants with a "collar" of cardboard or a juice can with top and bottom cut off).

Bees. Gardeners are sometimes puzzled by crescent-shaped holes in the edges of leaves of such plants as roses, because they can't find any beetles or worms on which to place the blame. Such damage may be caused by species of leaf-cutting bees that gnaw out wafers of greenery and stuff their nests with them. Fortunately, the damage they cause is usually minor.

Commonly found pests of plants

Chewing Insects and Larvae

(larvae are the immature form of various species of moths and butterflies)
Beetles
Caterpillars and other larvae and worms, including cutworms and borers.
Earwigs
Grasshoppers

Common Sucking Insects and Mites

Aphids or plant lice
Leaf hoppers or white flies
Thrips
Squash bugs
Midges
Red spider mites

Slugs and snails are not related to insects and are generally killed with special chemical sprays or metaldehyde baits.

INSECTICIDES

Insects can multiply rapidly. Cool, damp weather can cause a population explosion of aphids (plant lice). Prolonged hot, dry, dusty weather can bring an infestation of mites. Good gardeners make the rounds of their gardens at least twice weekly, inspecting new growth, the undersides of leaves, and the color and condition of foliage. Often, small "hot-spots" of insects or disease can be knocked out before they spread to other parts of the garden. Some gardeners find aerosol spray cans of insecticide handy for this purpose. (They are too expensive for large-scale use.)

Stomach and contact poisons. In former years insecticides could be classified rather neatly as "stomach poisons" or "contact poisons." Stomach poisons kill chewing insects that swallow the poisons along with plant tissue. Stomach poisons sometimes require a day or two to kill an insect. The residue on the plants usually lasts for two or three weeks, protecting plants with a thin film of poison. The poison may also act as a repellent, particularly when freshly applied. Contact poisons are used to kill sucking insects and mites by causing a rapid paralysis of the nervous system. Contact poisons leave minimal residues and must be applied fairly frequently to kill new broods of insect pests as they appear.

All-purpose insecticides. Modern insecticides are more difficult to classify. Some of the new, fast-acting contact poisons are lethal to beetles and caterpillars as well as to sucking insects. Certain of the long-lasting poisons that are designed primarily to kill chewing insects are also efficient against sucking types. Your best bet is to read labels to determine the class or classes of insects controlled by the product you are examining. Keep two formulas of insecticide handy, and use them alternately. This minimizes the genetic buildup of resistance in insects. You will find that many different brands contain similar concentrations of the same active ingredients, so look for *two different chemicals* that control the same classes of insects.

Your local nurseryman can be helpful in selecting insecticides, particularly those with low toxicity to humans. Some of the sophisticated new insecticides are not only highly efficient in killing insects, but also are dangerous to humans when swallowed or absorbed through the skin, particularly at full strength.

This book will not attempt to recommend specific chemicals, because improvements and new materials are appearing on the market so rapidly.

Systemic insecticides. The most modern method of control for pests is the systemic insecticide, which is applied to the soil or to the plant and spreads throughout its entire system. The pests that chew or suck the plant juices are killed. Systemics are poisonous to humans and pets and must be handled with great care. Presently available systemics should not be applied to vegetables (unless specifically recommended on the label) or to soils where vegetables are apt to be grown in the near future. Likewise, if systemics were applied, trimmings of treated flowers or the dead plants should not be composted if the compost is to be used on vegetables.

Systemic materials offer great promise. One granular kind is especially recommended for roses; others can be diluted, poured on the soil under plants, and watered in.

Biological control. Slow progress is being made in the use of "biological control" of insects. Products are available that consist of spores or "eggs" of bacteria harmless to humans but deadly when they sprout within the gut of a caterpillar. A similar product controls Japanese Beetles. Federal and state agencies occasionally release predatory or parasitic insects over large areas, but this is not something the home gardener can control.

PLANT DISEASES

Leaf or blossom diseases caused by fungi can disfigure plants. Mildew and rust diseases are widely distributed; rarely does a garden completely escape the ravages of one or the other. The injury is caused by the growth of spores (egglike reproductive bodies) that blow through the air, and land on foliage or are splashed up with soil particles by driving rain. These spores sprout and grow into various molds or other diseases that penetrate the outer surface of the plant and grow rootlike structures inside the stems and leaves. (You know they are there because of the gray, black, or reddish fruiting bodies that form on the surfaces of leaves and stems.)

Enlarged cross-section representation of leaf, showing cellular structure. Fungi such as mildew can enter through either upper or lower surfaces. Both surfaces must be sprayed or dusted to prevent or control fungous diseases.

Spores or fruiting bodies of the fungus
Outer cell layer
Spongy inner cells
Outer cell layer

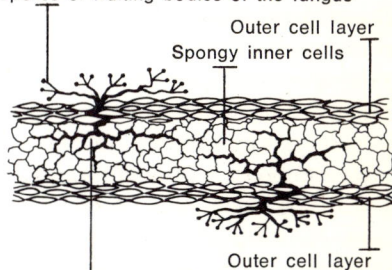

Threadlike fungus spreading inside the leaf cells

Fungous disease control. Fungous diseases can be controlled by sprays and dusts if both upper and lower surfaces of the leaves are covered. Disease control depends on spraying or dusting *before* the problem becomes serious—in other words, a preventive program. Spraying or dusting after diseases become entrenched rarely cures the problem, because parts of the disease organisms continue to work under the skin of plants, safe from poison sprays. Because new spores con-

43

tinue to be blown in, a regular preventive program must be set up to keep the plants fully protected. However, disease organisms, like insects, can build up a tolerance if you use only one kind of material for control. Two materials, used alternately, keep the organisms off balance.

Systemic fungicides. Systemic fungicides with long-lasting effects are now being introduced. They appear to have great promise for controlling mildew, rusts, and other serious fungous diseases.

Dormant spraying. Many gardeners, even those with long experience, neglect the most effective preventive measure for reducing disease problems on woody plants—that of "dormant spraying." Dormant spraying is accomplished when plants have shed their leaves. Dormant sprays kill not only disease spores on and around plants, but also many of the insects hiding under the bark and in the cracks of woody plants. When combined with a thorough cleanup of old leaves and other litter around plants, domant spraying sends plants into the spring with clean, healthy new growth. Furthermore, dormant spraying of woody plants kills many insects that also feed on flower gardens.

Viruses. Plant diseases caused by viruses are difficult to control. Viruses are usually carried by insects; they stunt plants, turn leaves yellow, and may eventually kill. The best preventive for virus diseases is control of the insects that carry and transmit them. Aphids and leaf hoppers are among the carriers. Once a plant has been infected with a virus disease (which can cause mottling or downward cupping of leaves) you should destroy it before the disease spreads.

Root rots and wilts. Unlike viruses, which ordinarily act rather slowly to weaken or kill a plant, certain other systemic diseases may travel rapidly throughout the entire system of a plant. Root rots and bacterial wilts clog the circulatory system and may kill plants rather quickly. Present-day chemicals are largely ineffective when applied after the disease has progressed enough to cause symptoms such as wilting. One good preventive for diseases transmitted through the soil is healthy, well-drained earth, liberally fortified with a good balance of plant foods and organic matter. A further precaution is crop rotation, never replanting the same kind of plant in the same bed two years in succession.

Natural resistance. Plant breeders are steadily increasing the natural resistance of flowers to epidemic diseases; in some cases, new varieties are entirely immune to certain diseases. Yet, new diseases or virulent new strains of well-known maladies are constantly developing or being introduced, and some disease organisms are building up an immunity to the older spray materials. The fight goes on increasingly!

SPRAY OR DUST?

Dusts are handy, because all you have to do is to shake a little into a duster and blow it on plants. There is no mess to clean up. Dusts are wasteful when compared to sprays, because relatively little of the dust is actually deposited on leaves and stems. Dusts should not be applied except when the air is still. Dusts are more difficult to apply to the undersides of leaves than are sprays and may discolor plants.

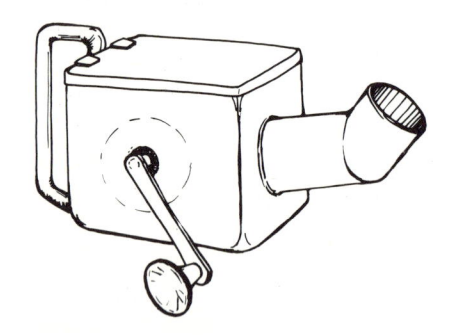

Lightweight, convenient crank-driven duster. Nozzle can be rotated 360 degrees to dust the undersides of leaves.

Sprays require more elaborate preparation and equipment than dusts, but savings in cost of materials can soon pay for the equipment. Sprays can completely cover plants, particularly the undersides of leaves and inside tightly compressed new growth. Sprays must be used with more care than dusts; for instance, sprays may burn leaf margins if applied during the heat of the day. And they should be used only when there is little wind.

In my experience, the handiest pieces of equipment are a small turbine-driven duster and a one- to three-gallon tank-type sprayer. These small pieces are easy to carry and simple to maintain. True, they must be refilled more often than larger units, but their portability offsets this disadvantage except in large gardens. Women prefer the one-gallon size; the three-gallon size can weigh about thirty pounds when filled.

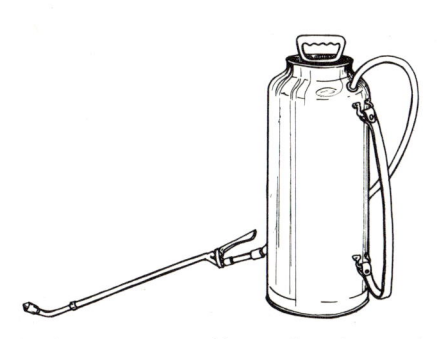

Tank-type sprayer with carrying strap and elbow nozzle that can reach under leaves.

Miscellaneous pests. Rabbits and deer may be furry and lovable in the wild, but in your garden they are implacable enemies. There are published lists of trees and shrubs that deer won't eat unless driven to it by starvation. You can loosely wrap the base of the trunks of trees and shrubs with hardware cloth or wire mesh to prevent rabbit damage. There are a few effective repellents to keep animals from nibbling annuals, bulbs, and perennials. Blood-meal and tankage work, after a fashion, and several proprietary repellents are now offered. A good bet is a tight, high fence with an outside border of dense, tall shrubs to discourage deer from jumping over.

Gophers and moles can be controlled by trapping. There are more elaborate devices, but trapping has provided the most reliable method. There is no way to eliminate gophers and moles for good unless the neighbors cooperate by setting traps in the runways of these pests.

POLLUTION DAMAGE

Certain plants are good "indicators" of air pollution. White varieties of petunias develop large bleached spots on their foliage when subjected to levels of smog that are high enough to cause smarting of eyes. Until our civilization learns to control air pollution, plants and humans alike will suffer increasing problems because plants also need to "breathe."

POISON: BEWARE!

There have been too many cases of sickness caused by garden poisons to underestimate their potency. The manufacturers warn against misuse, but gardeners become complacent. Here are a few common-sense precautions to follow, even with chemicals having a low mammalian toxicity:

1. Keep children and pets indoors when you are spraying or dusting.
2. Store insecticides, fungicides, and herbicides in a locked cabinet.
3. Do not transfer insecticides to other containers such as soft drink bottles or fruit jars.
4. Wear rubber or plastic gloves when measuring liquid insecticides.
5. Wash hands thoroughly with plenty of soap immediately after handling either liquids or dusts.
6. Stay out of spray drift; never spray or dust when the wind can blow it back on you.
7. Wear old clothes; immediately after spraying hang the old clothes outside and shower or bathe.

A spray can is ideal for applying weedkillers. The large, heavy drops are preferred to a fine, drifting spray from a pressure tank. Never use the same can for watering plants.

Weedkillers. Though weedkillers are not considered deadly poisons in the ordinary sense, they should be kept out of the reach of children because in concentrated form they can be hazardous. Also, anyone who has ever used his pressure-type sprayer for applying weedkillers can tell you how difficult it is to clean out the residue. Tiny contaminating remnants can remain and distort foliage when the sprayer is used even months later for insecticides or fungicides. Keep an old-fashioned sprinkling can for exclusive use in applying weedkillers. Label it for that use alone. Sprinkling cans have the added advantage of discharging the weedkilling solution in large droplets, which reduces damage due to spray drift.

Granular, long-lasting weedkillers have recently come on the market. These are good for killing most grasses and weeds in rose beds and along walls and walks. If you use them to suppress grass and weeds between plants of annual and perennial flowers, you run the chance of damaging your flowers. Until these materials have been further perfected, you would be better off using the tried and true method of cultivating to eliminate weeds in flower beds.

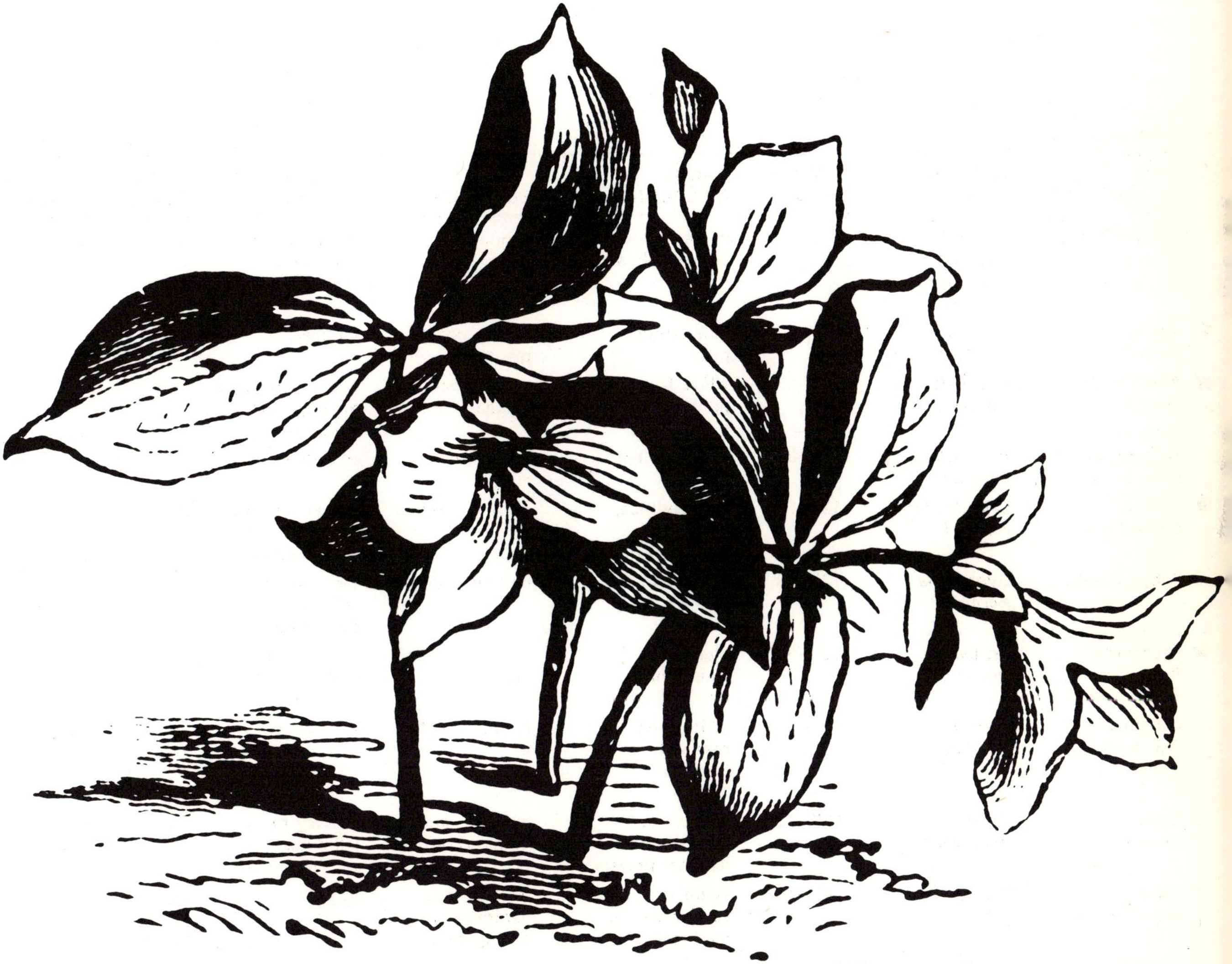

7 QUICK REFERENCE CHARTS OF PLANTS

ANNUALS

COMMON NAME	SCIENTIFIC NAME	APPROX. HEIGHT	RANGE OF COLORS	BEST USES	PEAK BLOOM SEASON	SUN OR SHADE	GROWN* FROM
African Daisy	Dimorphotheca sinuata, D. annuua & D. pluvialis	4"–16"	white, yellow orange, salmon	bedding in dry soils	winters where mild; early summer elsewhere	sun	S or V
★ Ageratum or Floss Flower	Ageratum houstonianum	4"–12"	blue, white, pink	edging, pot plant	summer, fall	sun	S
★ Alyssum, Sweet	Lobularia maritima	4"–8"	white, lavender, purple, rosy-pink	edging, rock garden	year-round where mild, spring to fall elsewhere	sun	S
Amaranthus or Love-lies-bleeding	Amaranthus caudatus	36"–84"	red tassel-like fronds	background	all summer	sun	S
★ Aster or China Aster	Callisthephus chinensis	12"–36"	lavender-blue, white, pink rose, crimson	cutting, bedding	late spring where mild; late summer elsewhere	sun	S
Baby's Breath	Gypsophila elegans	12"–18"	white, pink, rose	cutting, drying	early summer to fall, but of short duration	sun	S
★ Bachelor's Button or Cornflower	Centaurea cyanus	12"–30"	blue, pink, wine, white	cutting, bedding, drying	spring where mild; summer elsewhere	sun	S
Balsam or Touch-me-not	Impatiens balsaminea	8"–30"	white, pink, rose, red, lavender	bedding, cutting	summer to fall	light shade, or sun where cool	S
Basil, Ornamental	Ocimum 'Dark Opal'	12"–16"	bronzy, dark purple leaves, lavender flowers	bedding, dark foliage accents	summer to fall if seeds are sheared off	sun	S
Baby Blue-eyes	Nemophila mensiesii	6"–10"	white, with blue centers and tip markings	rock gardens, naturalizing among shrubs	spring	sun or light shade	S

*Legend: S=Seeds, V=Vegetative divisions

ANNUALS

	COMMON NAME	SCIENTIFIC NAME	APPROX. HEIGHT	RANGE OF COLORS	BEST USES	PEAK BLOOM SEASON	SUN OR SHADE	GROWN* FROM
★	Begonia, Fibrous-rooted or Wax Begonia	Begonia semperflorens	6"–18"	white, pink, deep rose, red	edging, bedding, containers	all summer	sun where cool; light shade elsewhere	S or V
	Bells of Ireland	Molucella laevis	18'–30'	green, bell-like bracts resembling flowers	cutting, drying	summer	sun	S
	Blanket Flower	Gaillardia pulchella	12"–24"	Doubled flowers in warm shades; wine, maroon	cutting, bedding	all summer	sun	S
	Blue Lace Flower	Trachymene caerulea	18'–24"	blue to violet-blue	cutting, drying	late spring or fall	sun	S
★	Calendula or Pot Marigold	Calendula officinalis	12"–24"	cream, yellow, orange, apricot	cutting, bedding	winters where mild; late spring elsewhere	sun	S
★	California Poppy	Eschscholzia californica	12"–18"	Gold, yellow, orange are usual; 'Mission Bells' includes pink & rose bicolors	bedding, naturalizing	winter & spring where mild; summer elsewhere	sun	S
	Calliopsis	Coreopsis tinctoria	8"–36"	Yellow, orange, maroon in zoned and splashed bicolors	bedding, dry soil	late spring to summer; through summer where cool	sun	S
	Candytuft	Iberis umbellata	8'–18'	Pastel pink, lavender, rose, lilac, salmon, white	bedding, cutting	late spring	sun	S
	Candytuft, Hyacinth Flowered	Iberis amara	12"–20"	Spikes, white only	cutting, fragrance	late spring	sun	S
★	Celosia or Plume Celosia	Celosia plumosa	12"–36"	pink, red, gold, yellow	bedding, background, cutting, drying	summer through fall, except where quite hot	sun	S
	Clarkia or Mountain Garland	Clarkia unguiculata	12"–36"	Mixed: white, pink, rose, crimson, purple, salmon	bedding, cutting, drying	late spring to summer; through summer where cool	sun	S
★	Cockscomb	Celosia cristata	12"–36"	pink, red, gold, yellow	(same as Celosia)	(same as Celosia)	sun	S
★	Coleus	Coleus blumei	12"–24"	Grown for its variegated leaves	bedding in moist, lightly shaded areas, containers	midsummer through early fall	shade	S or V
★	Cosmos	Cosmos bipinnatus	48"–72"	White, pink, lavender, rose, purple	background, temporary shrubs	all summer	sun	S

49

ANNUALS

COMMON NAME	SCIENTIFIC NAME	APPROX. HEIGHT	RANGE OF COLORS	BEST USES	PEAK BLOOM SEASON	SUN OR SHADE	GROWN* FROM
Cosmos, Yellow	Cosmos sulphureus	48"–84"	Yellow, orange, scarlet-orange	background	late summer	sun	S
Cupflower or Baby-blue-eyes	Nierembergia hippomanica caerulea	6"–12"	Blue to violet-blue	containers, edgings, hanging baskets	summer	sun	S
Delphinium, Annual	Delphinium grandiflorum	18"–24"	Blue shades	cutting	early summer	sun	S
Flowering Tobacco	Nicotiana alata & N. sanderae	18"–36"	Greenish-white, crimson, magenta	fragrance, cutting	all summer	light shade or sun	S
Forget-me-not	Myosotis sylvatica	6"–12"	Blue with white eye, pink	edging, naturalizing, groundcover	spring through late fall except where quite hot	light shade or dappled sun	S
★ Four O'Clock	Mirabilis jalapa	24"–48"	red, yellow, pink, white, some with markings	temporary shrubs or hedges; withstands urban conditions	all summer	light shade or full sun	S or V
Globe Amaranth or Old Fashioned Bachelor Button	Gomphrena globosa	9"–36"	white, purple, crimson, violet, dull gold	bedding, cutting, drying	all summer; heat-resistant	sun	S
★ Gloriosa Daisy	Rudbeckia hybrid	24"–48"	yellow, orange, mahogany, many bicolors	background, cutting	all summer; heat-resistant	sun	S
Godetia	Clarkia amoena	18"–24"	mostly mixed: white, pink, salmon, lavender	bedding, cutting, naturalizing	late spring; summer where cool	sun	S
★ Impatiens or Sultana	Impatiens sultani & I. holstii	6"–30"	scarlet, mauve, coral, magenta, purple, pink, white	bedding in lightly shaded areas	summer through early fall	light to medium shade	S or V
Joseph's Coat	Amaranthus tricolor	48"–84"	bronzy-green crown foliage marked with cream & red	background, cutting	summer	sun	S
Larkspur	Delphinium ajacis	18"–60"	Blue, pink, lavender, rose, salmon, carmine, white	background, cutting, drying	late spring to early summer	sun	S
Lobelia	Lobelia erinus	2"–9"	Blue, violet, pink, white	edging, rock gardens, containers, hanging baskets	summer	sun	S
Love-in-a-Mist or Devil-in-a Bush	Nigella damascena	12"–24"	blue, white, rose-pink	bedding, cutting, drying	early summer or fall	sun	S

*Legend: S=Seeds, V=Vegetative divisions.

'Floral Carpet' snapdragons, mixed colors, with 'Violet Queen' alyssum, and 'Carpet of Snow' in foreground.
Courtesy T. Sakata & Co.

ANNUALS

COMMON NAME	SCIENTIFIC NAME	APPROX. HEIGHT	RANGE OF COLORS	BEST USES	PEAK BLOOM SEASON	SUN OR SHADE	GROWN* FROM
Lupin, Annual	Lupinus hartwegii	18"—36"	blue, white, pink	naturalizing	early summer	sun	S
★ Madascar Periwinkle	Catharanthus rosea	6"—36"	white, rose-pink, blush-pink	bedding; heat-resistant	all summer until early fall	sun	S
★ Marigold, African or American	Tagetes erecta and hybrids with other species	10"—48"	mostly yellow, orange, tangerine, gold	bedding, edging, background (depending on height), cutting	all summer, except where quite hot	sun	S
★ Marigold, French	Tagetes patula and hybrids with other species	6"—18"	like African; includes russet, mahogany & bicolors	bedding, edging	same as African, except earlier	sun	S
Mexican Sunflower	Tithonia rotundifolia	36"—84"	orange and orange-scarlet	background, cutting; forms a large shrub where warm	summer to fall very heat-resistant	sun	S
Mignonette	Reseda odorata	8"—18"	greenish-brown clusters	fragrance, containers	late spring until fall	sun	S
★ Moss Rose	Portulaca grandiflora	4"— 8"	satiny red, purple, cerise, rose-pink, yellow, orange, white	rock gardens; hot, dry, or sandy soil	all summer	sun	S
★ Nasturtium	Tropaeolum majus	12"—18" Some spread vigorously	white, pink, crimson, orange, maroon, yellow, bicolors	bedding, cutting	spring & fall; summer where cool	sun or light shade	S
Nemesia	Nemesia strumosa	10"—18"	all colors except green, many warm shades	containers, bedding	spring where mild; early summer elsewhere	sun	S
Painted Tongue	Salpiglossis sinuata	18"—36"	bizarre patterns of red, orange, yellow, pink, purple	background cutting	early summer	sun	S
★ Pansy	Viola tricolor hortensis	6"—10"	"faces" in white, yellow, purple, rose, mahogany, violet, apricot	edging; small containers	spring & fall; winter where mild	sun	S
★ Petunia	Petunia hybrida	12"—18"	all except true blue, yellow and orange	bedding, containers, hanging baskets, cutting	all summer & fall	sun	S
★ Phlox, Annual	Phlox drummondi	6"—24"	numerous bicolors; all shades except blue and gold	bedding, naturalizing	late spring & fall	sun	S
Pincushion Flower or Mourning Bride	Scabiosa atropurpurea	18"—48"	deep maroon, pink, salmon-pink, white	background cutting	summer	sun	S

*Legend: S=Seeds, V=Vegetative divisions.

ANNUALS

COMMON NAME	SCIENTIFIC NAME	APPROX. HEIGHT	RANGE OF COLORS	BEST USES	PEAK BLOOM SEASON	SUN OR SHADE	GROWN* FROM
★ Pinks or Dianthus	Dianthus species & hybrids	6"–30"	mostly bicolors of white, pink, lavender & purple	bedding, edging, cutting, fragrance	spring-fall; winter where mild	sun	S or V
Poppy, Shirley	Papaver rhoeas	18"–36"	red, pink, white, scarlet, salmon bicolors	background, naturalizing, cutting	late spring	sun	S
★ Salvia or Scarlet Sage	Salvia splendens	10"–36"	bright red, rose, lavender-pink	bedding, background	all summer & fall	sun	S
Scarlet Flax	Linum grandiflorum rubrum	12"–18"	scarlet to deep red, rose	bulb bed cover, quick bloom	late spring & fall	sun	S
Snapdragon	Antirrhinum majus	10"–48"	large choice of colors & blossom forms	bedding, cutting	late spring & fall; summers where cool	sun	S
Spiderflower	Cleome spinosa	36"–60"	shrimp-pink, white	temporary shrub or hedge	all summer & fall	sun	S
Statice	Limonium sinuata & L. bonduellii	18"–30"	blue, rose, lavender, yellow, bicolors with white	cutting, drying	summer	sun	S
Stock	Matthiola incana	12"–36"	white, cream, yellow, pink, rose, crimson-red, purple	edging, bedding, cutting, fragrance	winters where mild, late spring elsewhere	sun	S
Strawflower	Helichrysum bracteatum	24"–48"	mixed warm shades: yellow, bronze, orange, pink, white	cutting, drying, background	late summer-fall	sun	S
Summer Forget-Me-Not	Anchusa capensis	12"–18"	clean blue with white throat	bedding, naturalizing	summer	light shade or sun	S
Sunflower	Helianthus annuus	18" to 15 ft. or more	yellow & mahogany bicolors, or yellow with black center	screens, hedges, children's gardens	summer	sun	S
Sweet Pea, Winter-flowering	Lathyrus odorata	36"–72" Climber (new, low-growing varieties are available)	mixed or separate colors, all except yellow, orange, & green	special beds for cutting and fragrance	late winter where mild; not heat-resistant	sun	S
Sweet Pea, Summer-flowering	Same	Same	same	same	spring where mild, early summer elsewhere; somewhat heat-resistant	sun	S

53

ANNUALS

COMMON NAME	SCIENTIFIC NAME	APPROX. HEIGHT	RANGE OF COLORS	BEST USES	PEAK BLOOM SEASON	SUN OR SHADE	GROWN* FROM
Tagetes or Signet Marigold	*Tagetes tenuifolia (signata)*	10″–24″	small, numerous, yellow, orange	bedding, rock gardens, containers	all summer except where quite warm	sun	S
★ Verbena	*Verbena hybrida*	6″–12″	bright pink, scarlet, blue, purple, some bicolors	edging, bedding, groundcover	summer	sun	S
Viola or Tufted Pansy	*Viola cornuta*	6″– 8″	resembles pansies, except without distinct "faces"	edging, containers	winter where mild, spring & fall elsewhere	light shade or sun	S
Wishbone flower	*Torenia fournieri*	12″–16″	deep blue marked with yellow, white	bedding, containers	all summer	light shade or sun	S
★ Zinnia, Giant-flowered	*Zinnia elegans*	18″–36″	red, orange, yellow, purple, lavender, pink, white, green	bedding, cutting	all summer	sun	S
Zinnia, Mexican	*Zinnia angustifolia*	12″–18″	yellow, orange, white, maroon, mahogany	bedding, cutting, dry areas	all summer	sun	S
★ Zinnia, Small-flowered	*Zinnia elegans*	8″–36″	same as Giant-flowered	edging, bedding, cutting	all summer	sun	S

*Legend: S=Seeds, V=Vegetative divisions.

PERENNIALS AND BIENNIALS †

COMMON NAME	SCIENTIFIC NAME	APPROX.‡ HEIGHT	RANGE OF COLORS	BEST USES	PEAK BLOOM SEASON	SUN OR SHADE	GROWN* FROM
Adam's Needle	*Yucca filamentosa*	36''—72''	creamy white	dry knolls and hot corners; sandy or poor soil	late summer	full sun	S or V
Allium, Giant	*Allium giganteum*	18''—30'' (48''—60'' in West)	lilac	background	summer	sun	Bulb
★ Aster, Cushion	*Aster hybridus nanus*	9''—15''	mixed: most colors except yellow	edging	fall	sun	V
★ Aster, New England	*Aster novae-angliae*	36''—60''	blue, violet, pink, white	roadsides, background	fall	sun	S or V
Avens or Geum	*Geum chiloense*	to 24''	yellow, red, orange	bedding; contrast with blues	early summer	light shade	S or V
Baby's Breath	*Gypsophila paniculata*	24''—36''	white (small)	cutting, drying	early summer-summer	sun	S or V
Balloon-Flower	*Platycodon grandiflorum*	18''—24''	pink, white, purple, blue	background, cutting	mid- to late summer	sun	S or V
★ Basket of Gold or Hardy alyssum	*Alyssum saxatile 'Compactum'*	8''—12''	golden-yellow, tinged with chartreuse	streamsides or rockeries	early spring	sun	S or V
Beard Tongue	*Penstemon gloxinioides*, horticultural hybrids	18''—36''	blue, pink, crimson mostly bicolors	dry beds as a medium-height background	summer-fall	sun	S or V
Bee Balm	*Monarda 'Cambridge Scarlet'*	36''	scarlet-red, pink, white	cutting	summer-fall	sun	V
Bishop's hat	*Epimedium grandiflorum*	to 12'' vining	red, violet	woodsy groundcover	summer	light shade	V
★ Blanket-Flower	*Gaillardia aristata (grandiflora)*	24''—36''	yellow or bicolor with deep red	roadsides, dry banks	summer-fall	sun	S or V
Blazing Star or Gayfeather	*Liatris pycnostachya*	36''—48''	rosy-purple, white	background, cutting	late summer	sun	S or V
★ Bleeding Heart	*Dicentra spectabilis*	24''—36''	pink, rose, white	woodsy glades, cutting	spring	light shade	V
Bleeding Heart, Western	*Dicentra formosa*	8''—18''	pink, pale-rose, rosy-purple	woodsy underplantings	spring-fall	light shade	V
Blue Flax	*Linum perenne*	24''	sky blue	feathery, erect-growing groundcover	summer	sun	S
Blister-Cress or Siberian Wallflower	*Erysimum asperum*	12''—18''	golden-orange	bedding	spring	sun	S

† Unless specifically listed as "biennial," the plant is generally classed as perennial.
‡ All the heights listed are for plants grown under fairly long-season conditions such as prevail in the central Midwest. Where summers are short or the garden area is windy, perennials will grow only about three quarters as high as indicated.

PERENNIALS AND BIENNIALS

COMMON NAME	SCIENTIFIC NAME	APPROX. HEIGHT	RANGE OF COLORS	BEST USES	PEAK BLOOM SEASON	SUN OR SHADE	GROWN* FROM
Butterfly-Bush or Summer Lilac	Buddleia davidii	72"–120"	blue, rose, lilac	use as a tall shrub	summer	sun	V
★ Bugle or Bugle-Weed	Ajuga reptans	4"– 8"	bronze-green leaves, violet flowers	groundcover	summer	sun or shade	V
Butterfly-Weed	Asclepias tuberosa	24"–36"	orange-yellow	sandy, gravelly or dry beds or roadsides	summer	sun	S
★ Candytuft, Perennial	Iberis sempervirens	8"–12"	white	edgings, groundcover	early summer	sun	S
Canterbury Bells	Campanula medium calycanthema	24"–36"	violet, lavender, white, pink	background	early summer	sun	S
Carnation (see Dianthus)							
Carpathian Bellflower	Campanula carpatica	9"–12"	blue, white	rock walls, hanging baskets	summer	sun	S or V
Chinese Lantern	Physalis alkekengi	12"–24"	orange; inflated papery husks	containers (invasive) cutting, drying	fall	light shade or sun	S or V
★ Chives	Allium schoenoprasum	10"–12"	lavender-pink; cloverlike	decorative edging; leaves are edible	summer-fall	sun	S or V
Christmas Rose	Helleborus niger	To 18"	purplish-white	woodsy groundcover	winter & early spring	light shade	S or V
Chrysanthemum, Florists'	Chrysanthemum morifolrum	18"–30"	most colors except blue	bedding, cutting	late summer-fall	sun	V
Chrysanthemum, Cushion	Chrysanthemum morifolrum	12"–18"	most colors except blue	bedding, containers	summer-fall	sun	V
Columbine, Dwarf	Aquilegia alpina	To 12"	blue	roadsides & rockeries	early summer	sun or light shade	S or V
★ Columbine, Long-Spurred	Aquilegia, 'Mckana's'	24"–48"	mixed colors; mostly bicolors	background, medium to large rockeries	early summer	sun or light shade	S or V
★ Coral Bells	Heuchera sanguinea	12"–18" (24" in West)	red, pink, white	spacious rockeries, edging, cutting	early summer	sun or light shade	S or V
Cranesbill	Geranium grandiflorum	To 12"	blue, marked with red	rockeries or edging	summer	light shade	S or V
Cranesbill	Geranium sanguineum	12"–18"	rose, pink, purple, white	rockeries or edging	summer	light shade	S or V
★ Day-lily	Hemerocallis, horticultural hybrids	12"–72"	most colors except blue, green, violet, true red	bedding & cutting	midsummer to fall, depending on variety	sun or light shade	V
★ Delphinium, 'Connecticut Yankees'	Delphinium, horticultural hybrid	24"–36"	blue, violet, white	cutting, low backgrounds	early summer	sun	S or V

56

PERENNIALS AND BIENNIALS

COMMON NAME	SCIENTIFIC NAME	APPROX. HEIGHT	RANGE OF COLORS	BEST USES	PEAK BLOOM SEASON	SUN OR SHADE	GROWN* FROM
Delphinium, 'Pacific Giants'	Delphinium, horticultural hybrid	48"—60"	blue, white, lavender-pink	vertical accents in background plantings	early summer	sun	S or V
Dianthus 'Alwoodii'	Dianthus	To 12"	white, pink, crimson	rockeries, edging, cutting	spring only	sun	V
English Daisy	Bellis perennis	3"— 6"	white, pink, rose	rockeries, edging, naturalizing	spring, winter where mild	sun	S or V
Euphorbia veneta (wulfenii)	same	24"—36"	bluish foliage, yellow flowers fleshy leaves	containers	early summer; winter where mild	sun	S or V
European Pasque-Flower	Anemone pulsatilla	9"—15"	lavender-to-violet	background	spring	sun or light shade	S or V
False Dragon Head	Physostegia virginiana	36"—60"	white & rose bicolors	streamsides, background, cutting (spreads rapidly)	midsummer to late summer	sun	S or V
False Indigo	Baptisia australis	30"—72"	indigo-blue	background, decorative pods	summer	sun	S
Fernleaf Yarrow	Achillea filipendulina	48"—60"	chrome yellow	background, cutting, drying	summer-fall	sun	S or V
★ Forget-me-not Anchusa	Brunnera macrophylla	12"—18"	blue	bulb bed cover and under shrubs	spring and summer	light shade	S or V
Foxglove, Common, 'Excelsior'	Digitalis purpurea	48"—96"	pink, white, purple, yellow bicolors	background & around tree trunks	early summer	sun or partial shade	S
Foxglove, Dwarf 'Foxy'	Digitalis purpurea hybrid	18"—30"	mixed colors, marked and spotted	bedding	early summer	partial shade or sun	S
Fringed Wormwood	Artemisia frigida	12"—18"	silvery-white, finely cut leaves	rockeries	summer-fall	sun	V
Globe-Flower	Trollius europaeus	24"—36"	yellow	damp soil, background	early summer	light shade	V
Globe Thistle	Echinops exaltatus	36"—48"	steel-blue	cutting	late summer	sun	S or V
Golden marguerite	Anthemis tinctoria 'Kelwayi'	24"—36"	yellow	background	summer-fall	sun	S or V
Goutweed or Bishop's Weed	Aegopodium podagraria	12'—24"	green & white leaves	groundcover, spreads rapidly (invasive)	all summer	sun or shade	V
Heartleaf Bergenia	Bergeoia cordifolia	12"—18"	white, rose	rockeries, groundcovers	early summer	sun or light shade	V
Heliopsis	Heliopsis scabra	36"—48"	orange & yellow	background & cutting	summer-fall	sun	S

*Legend: S=Seeds, V=Vegetative divisions.

PERENNIALS AND BIENNIALS

COMMON NAME	SCIENTIFIC NAME	APPROX. HEIGHT	RANGE OF COLORS	BEST USES	PEAK BLOOM SEASON	SUN OR SHADE	GROWN* FROM
★ Hens and Chickens	Sempervivum tectorum and other species	2"– 4"	gray-green rosettes, orange-pink flower spikes	containers, rockeries, edging	summer-fall	light shade or full sun	V
★ Hollyhock	Althea rosea	48"–108"	most colors except true blue and green	backgrounds or fence corners, cutting	summer	sun	S or V
★ Iris, Bearded or German	Iris pogoniria group	Mostly 24" to 48"; dwarfs from 3"–12"	most except scarlet and true green	display beds, cutting; dwarfs for edgings	early summer; spring where mild	sun	V
Iris Moss	Sagina subulata (Arenaria verna caespitosa)	1"– 3"	mossy green carpet; small white flowers	between flag-stones, in rockeries	summer-fall	sun or light shade	S or V
Japanese Anemone	Anemone hupenhensis japonica	24"–48"	white, pink, rose	streamsides, under trees; borders	fall	sun or light shade	V
★ Japanese Spurge	Pachysandra terminalis	6"– 8"	green foliage, white flowers, inconspicuous	groundcover	clean green foliage all year-round	light to deep shade	V
Lavender	Lavandula spica	24"–48"	purple-blue	cutting, drying	summer	sun	S or V
Leopard's Bane	Doronicum caucasicum 'Magnificum'	18"–24"	yellow	bedding, cutting	early summer to fall	light shade	V
Lily-of-the-valley	Convallaria majalis	9"–12"	white, pink	fragrant groundcover in moist areas	spring-early summer	light to medium shade	V
★ Lily	Lilium, Horticultural hybrids and species	12"–84"	white, pink, yellow, mahogany, orange, gold with bicolors	vertical accents in perennial borders	early summer	full sun to light shade	V
Lupin	Lupinus 'Russell's' or "Royal"	18"–48"	mixed colors; pink, blue, & yellow combinations	bedding, background	summer	sun or light shade	S or V
Maiden Pink	Dianthus deltoides	8"–12"	rose, pink, white	rockeries & rock walls	early summer	sun	S or V
Mullein Pink	Lychnis coronaria	18"–30"	magenta, white, deep-crimson; gray foliage	rockeries & other beds that get little attention	summer-fall	sun	S or V
Myrtle Euphorbia	Euphorbia myrsinites	8"–15"	chartreuse-yellow	mixed with other succulents	spring-summer	sun	S or V
Painted Daisy	Chrysanthemum coccineum	24"–36"	white, pink, red	cutting	early summer	sun	S or V
Peachleaf Bluebell	Campanula persicifolia	24"–36"	white, pink, blue	background, perennial borders	summer	sun or light shade	S

*Legend: S=Seeds, V=Vegetative divisions.

58

PERENNIALS AND BIENNIALS

COMMON NAME	SCIENTIFIC NAME	APPROX. HEIGHT	RANGE OF COLORS	BEST USES	PEAK BLOOM SEASON	SUN OR SHADE	GROWN* FROM
★ Peony	Paeonia, Horticultural hybrids	18″–48″	white, pink, crimson, lavender, cream	cutting, bedding	early summer	light shade or sun	S or V
Phlox, Blue	Phlox divaricata	To 12″	blue, white, pink, rose	wall gardens, bulb bed covers	early spring	light shade or sun	V
★ Phlox, Creeping or Moss Phlox; also Moss Pink	Phlox subulata	To 6″	lavender-blue, scarlet, cerise, white	groundcover, rockeries	late spring	sun	V
★ Phlox, Perennial or Summer Phlox	Phlox paniculata	24″–48″	pink, purple, rose, white, orange, scarlet	backgrounds, mixed in perennial borders, cutting	late summer-fall	sun	V
Pincushion Flower, Perennial	Scabiosa caucasica	24″–30″	white, blue, purple	bedding, cutting	summer-fall	sun	S or V
★ Plantain-Lily, Fragrant or Funkia	Hosta plantaginea (subcordata)	24″–36″	white with light, yellow-green leaves	shady borders, containers, moist areas, pond banks	late summer	light to heavy shade	V
Plantain-Lily, Variegated or Funkia	Hosta decorata (marginata)	To 24″	lavender, with variegated leaves	shaded borders, streamsides, containers	early summer	light to heavy shade	V
Poppy-flowered Anemone	Anemone coronaria 'St. Brigid'	To 18″	rich colors, mostly mixed	rockeries, cut flowers	spring	sun	Tuber
Poppy Mallow	Callirhoe involucrata	To 12″	rose, purple	dry rockeries	summer-fall	sun	S
Poppy, Oriental	Papaver orientale	24″–48″	pink, white, scarlet, salmon	cutting, bedding, in perennial borders	early summer	sun	S or V
Primrose, Evening or Showy Evening Primrose	Oenothera erythrosepala (lamarckiana)	36″–60″	bright yellow	evening bloom	summer	sun	S or V
Primrose, Mexican	Oenothera speciosa childsii	10″–16″	white to rose-pink, butter-yellow pollen	meadows, roadsides, naturalizing	summer	sun	S or V
★ Primrose, English	Primula polyantha horticultural hybrids	10″–14″	mixed and bicolors; spectacular blues, yellows, reds	edgings, underplantings between shrubs	late spring; winter where mild	light shade	S or V
Rock-cress	Aubretia deltoidea	6″–10″	violet, pink, purple	rock walls, rock gardens	early summer	sun	S or V
Salvia, Gentian or Blue Salvia	Salvia patens	24″–36″	deep blue to true blue	bedding, cutting, not hardy in the far north	summer-fall	sun	S or V
Saxifrage 'London Pride'	Saxifraga umbrosa	12″–18″	white, pink, bicolors	pots, wall gardens, edgings	early summer	light shade	V
Sea-Holly	Eryngium amethystinum	18″–24″	steel blue, followed by spiny pods	cutting, drying	late summer	sun	S or V

PERENNIALS AND BIENNIALS

COMMON NAME	SCIENTIFIC NAME	APPROX. HEIGHT	RANGE OF COLORS	BEST USES	PEAK BLOOM SEASON	SUN OR SHADE	GROWN* FROM
Sea-Lavender	Limonium latifolium	24"–36"	blue-white, variegated	cutting, drying	summer-fall	sun	S
Sea-Pink or Thrift	Armeria maritima	To 12"	purple, pink, white	oceansides, edging, tops of walls, rockeries	spring-summer	sun	S
★ Shasta Daisy	Chrysanthemum maximum	24"–30"	white	background, cutting	summer-fall	sun	S or V
Showy Sedum	Sedum spectabile	12"–24"	rose to carmine	rockeries, containers, dry soil	late summer-fall	sun	V
Sneeze-Weed	Helenium autumnale	36"–48"	orange, yellow, rusty bicolors	backgrounds, cutting	summer-fall	sun	S
★ Snow-in-summer	Cerastium tomentosum	6'–12"	white, with gray foliage	rockeries, wall gardens; spreads rapidly	early summer	sun	S or V
Speedwell	Veronica, horticultural hybrids	24"–36"	blue, pink, white, lavender	slender, spikey accents, cutting	midsummer	light shade or sun	V
Stokes' Aster	Stokesia laevis	12"–24"	blue, white, lavender	bedding, cutting	late summer	sun	S or V
Stonecrop	Sedum sieboldii	To 8"	pink, coppery fall foliage	pots, hanging baskets, rockeries	late summer-fall	light shade or sun	V
Sweet Rocket (Biennial)	Hesperis matronalis	24"–36"	white, lavender	background, cutting, quaint flower	early summer	sun or light shade	S
Sweet Pea, Perennial	Lathyrus latifolius	Vine	pink, white, lavender	groundcover, screening	early summer	sun	S
★ Sweet Violet	Viola odorata	6"–12"	white, blue, lavender, pink	groundcover, containers, cutflowers	spring	moderate shade	V
Sweet William (Biennial)	Dianthus barbatus	6"–24"	white, pink; zoned and edged	among shrubs, in perennial borders; tall varieties may be cut	early summer	sun or light shade	S
Summer Forget-me-not (Biennial)	Anchusa capensis	12"–18"	pure, bright blue (beautiful with sweet William)	bedding in lightly shaded areas; good blue summer flower	early summer	sun or light shade	S
Thermopsis	Thermopsis caroliniana	36"–48"	yellow spikes	tall accents	midsummer	sun	S
★ Tickseed	Coreopsis grandiflora 'Sunburst'	18"–30"	golden yellow	bedding, cutting	summer	sun (heat-resistant)	S
★ Virginia Bluebells	Mertensia virginica	To 18"	bicolor blue-pink	woodland undergrowth or shaded borders	early spring	light shade	V

PERENNIALS AND BIENNIALS

COMMON NAME	SCIENTIFIC NAME	APPROX. HEIGHT	RANGE OF COLORS	BEST USES	PEAK BLOOM SEASON	SUN OR SHADE	GROWN* FROM
Wall Rock-cress	*Arabis caucasica*	4"–10"	white	chinked into walls or rocks	early spring	sun or light shade	S
Willow Gentian	*Gentiana asclepiadea*	To 24"	blue to violet	woodlands or rockeries in high shade	late summer	light shade	S or V
Wormwood	*Artemisia albula* 'Silver King'	24"–48"	silvery-gray foliage	good blender, foliage color accents; cutting	summer-fall	sun	V
Yarrow or Sneezewort	*Achillea ptarmica* 'Perry's White'	To 18"	white	bedding, drying	summer-fall	sun	V
Yarrow or Milfoil	*Achillea millefolium* 'Fire King'	18"–24"	deep rose	bedding, drying	summer-fall	sun	V

*Legend: S=Seeds, V=Vegetative divisions.

TENDER PERENNIALS

COMMON NAME	SCIENTIFIC NAME	APPROX. HEIGHT	RANGE OF COLORS	BEST USES	PEAK BLOOM SEASON	SUN OR SHADE	GROWN* FROM
★ Amaryllis, Giant	Hippeastrum hybridum	18"–24"	orange, red, white, bicolors	pots or window boxes	summer	light shade or sun	B
Basket Flower	Hymenocallis calathina	24"	white	containers, or with blue flowers	early summer	sun	B
★ Begonia, Tuberous Rooted	Begonia tuberhybrida	12"–24"	red, white, yellow, pink, orange, picotee	containers, hanging baskets, raised beds	late summer-fall	light shade	T
Belladonna Lily	Amaryllis belladonna	24"–36"	rose-pink, white	dry banks, or along rustic fences	late summer	sun	B
Blue Marguerite	Felecia amelloides	to 18"	sky blue	parking strips, walks	summer	sun	V
Caladium	Caladium bicolor	12"–36"	large, fancy, vari-colored leaves	pots or planters	summer	afternoon shade	T
★ Calla	Zantedeschia	12"–24"	white, yellow, pink, orange, lavender	moist beds	summer	light shade	S or V
★ Canna or Indian Shot	Canna	36"–72"	all but blue and violet	background	summer-fall	sun	R or S
Cape Marigold	Dimorphotheca ecklonis	24"–36"	lavender-white	cutting, bedding	early summer-fall	sun	S
★ Clove Pink or Carnation	Dianthus caryophyllus Fragrance	12"–18"	white, pink, crimson, peach	edging	early summer	sun	S or V
★ Dahlia Named Cultivars	Dahlia	36"–84"	all except blue	in special display beds	late summer-fall	sun	T
★ Dwarf Dahlia, Unwin's	Dahlia	24"–36"	mixed	cutting, bedding	late summer-fall	sun	S or T
★ Dusty Miller	Centaurea gymnocarpa	18"–24"	velvety-white, decorative foliage	foliage accents	summer	sun	S
Feverfew or Matricaria	Chrysanthemum parthenium White Stars	to 15"	white	edging	summer-fall	sun	S
Florists Cyclamen	Cyclamen persicum	6"–12"	white, pink, rose, crimson	underplantings for trees and shrubs	late winter-spring	light shade	T
Foxtail Lily	Eremurus himalaicus	to 84"	cream yellow	background	early spring	sun	S or V
Freesia, Hybrids	Freesia	18"–24"	rose, mauve, white, yellow, orange	among shrubs or naturalizing	spring where mild	sun	C
★ Gazania	Gazania parviflora Copper King	12"	yellow & brown bicolors	parking strips and groundcovers	summer; fall & spring where mild	sun	V
Gerbera or Transvaal Daisy	Gerbera jamesonii	18"	pink, cerise, white, yellow, scarlet	bedding, cutting	spring, fall	sun	S or V

TENDER PERENNIALS

COMMON NAME	SCIENTIFIC NAME	APPROX. HEIGHT	RANGE OF COLORS	BEST USES	PEAK BLOOM SEASON	SUN OR SHADE	GROWN* FROM
★ Geranium, 'Lady Washington'	*Pelargonium domesticum*	18"–48"	wider choice than common geranium	bedding containers, groundcover	summer-fall	sun	V
Geranium, Ivy	*Pelargonium peltatum*	Vining	white, pink, rose, red, lavender	groundcover, hanging baskets, walls	summer, fall	sun	V
★ Gladiolus	*Gladiolus hortulanus*	18"–24"	most except blue	display beds, cutting	early summer	sun	C
Glory Lily	*Gloriosa rothschildiana*	Weak climber	crimson, white	large containers	midsummer	sun	T
Heliotrope	*Heliotropum arborescens*	18"–36"	violet, blue, white	cutting, bedding, fragrance	summer	light shade or sun	S or V
Iceland Poppy	*Papaver nudicaule*	12"–24"	yellow, orange, salmon, pink, white	bedding, cutting	winter where mild, late spring elsewhere	sun	S or V
Kafir Lily	*Clivia miniata*	18"–24"	red, white, yellow orange	containers, bedding in high shade	late winter-spring	sun or light shade	T
Ladies' Purse	*Calceolaria crenatiflora*	12"–24"	warm shades, nice markings	containers, bedding	summer	light shade	S or V
★ Lily-of-the-Nile	*Agapanthus africanus*	18"–48"	blue, white	display plants, large containers	midsummer	sun	T or S
Lily Turf, Big Blue	*Liriope muscari*	18"	violet-blue	edgings, containers	summer	light shade	S or V
★ Marguerite	*Chrysanthemum frutescens*	24"–48"	white, yellow, pink	seaside gardens, cutting, background	summer; year-round where mild	sun	V
Persian Ranunculus	*Ranunculus asiaticus*	12"–18"	mixed colors	containers, bedding, cutting	spring	sun	T
Pride of Madeira	*Echium fastuosum*	48"–72"	blue-purple	shrublike, backgrounds, seaside plantings	early summer	sun	S or V
★ Red Hot Poker or Torch Lily	*Kniphofia uvaria*	24"–72"	cream, white, yellow, orange-red	tall accents, dry beds, seaside gardens	early summer	sun	V
Wallflower	*Cheiranthus cheiri*	12"–30"	yellow, orange, bronze	wall gardens, rockeries	early summer	sun	S

*Legend: S=Seeds, V=Vegetative divisions, B=Bulbs, T=Tubers, R=Rhizomes, C=Corms

SPRING BULBS

COMMON NAME	SCIENTIFIC NAME	APPROX. HEIGHT	RANGE OF COLORS	BEST USES	PEAK BLOOM SEASON	SUN OR SHADE	GROWN* FROM
Daffodils (see Narcissus)							
★ Crocus, or Dutch Crocus	*Crocus vernus*	3"– 6"	white, yellow, lavender, purple, often streaked	in drifts under shrubs and on hillsides	very early spring	sun	C (small)
Glory-of-the-snow	*Chionodoxia*	4"– 6"	blue or violet	rock gardens or under shrubs for early bloom	very early spring	sun or light shade	B (small)
Grape Hyacinth	*Muscari*	4"– 8"	blue or white	naturalized on hillsides or under shrubs in drifts	early spring	sun or light shade	B (small)
★ Hyacinth or Dutch Hyacinth	*Hyacinthus*	6"–12"	blue, violet, pink, lavender, white, crimson	edgings, rock gardens, containers	early spring	sun	B (med.)
Iris reticulata or Violet-scented Iris	Same	6"– 8"	violet, tinged with gold	tufts for pots or woodland naturalizing	early spring	light shade	B (small)
★ Narcissus or Daffodil	*Narcissus species* and cultivars	6"–24"	white, yellow, orange, cream, apricot; many with contrasting "cups"	pot plant, naturalizing, special beds, among shrubs	early to midspring	sun	B (rather large)
Scilla or squill	*Scilla*	6"–24"	blue	scattered among shrubs, naturalized	early to midspring	sun	B (small)
Snowdrops	*Galanthus*	6"–12"	white	scattered among shrubs, naturalized in drifts	very early spring	sun or light shade	B (small)
Snowflake	*Leucojum*	9"–18"	white, pendent	naturalizing in moist spots	very early spring	sun or light shade	B (small)
Trillium or Wakerobin	*Trillium*	12"–24"	white or rose (dull)	naturalizing in in woodsy glens	midspring	light to medium sun	R
★ Tulip	*Tulipa*	10"–36"	most colors except blue; many bicolors, unusual species	special beds or containers; species tulips often naturalized	mid- to late spring	sun	B (rather large)
Winter Aconite	*Eranthis*	4"– 8"	yellow	under shrubs, shady banks	late winter or early spring	light to medium shade	S or T

*Legend: S=Seeds, V=Vegetative divisions, B=Bulbs, T=Tubers, R=Rhizomes, C=Corms

WATER PLANTS AND BOG PLANTS

COMMON NAME	SCIENTIFIC NAME	APPROX. HEIGHT	RANGE OF COLORS	BEST USES	PEAK BLOOM SEASON	SUN OR SHADE	GROWN* FROM
Astilbe (False Spirea or Meadow Sweet)	*Astilbe*	6"–36"	pink, white, red	poolsides, stream banks, pots & tubs	early to midsummer	light shade	V
Cattail	*Typha*	24"–60"	brown mature cattails	ponds, bogs, shallow streams	late summer	sun	Rootstocks
Cardinal Flower	*Lobelia cardinalis*	24"–48"	flame red	on mounds of soil in bogs	midsummer	sun or light shade	S
Hibiscus or Swamp Mallow	*Hibiscus moscheotus*	48"–72"	white, pink, red, bicolors	edges of ponds; any heavy, moist soil	all summer	sun	S or V
★ Japanese Iris	*Iris kaempferi*	24"–48"	purple, rose, red, white, pink	edges of pools or streams	midsummer	sun	R
Lotus	*Nelumbo*	Blooms on surface of water	yellow, white, rose	in boxes of soil 18" below surface of water	midsummer	sun	Rootstocks
Lythrium	*Lythrium salicaria*	30"–60"	lavender, pink, magenta	moist soil, anywhere	midsummer thru fall	sun	V
Marsh Marigold	*Caltha palustris*	12"–24"	bright yellow	on soil hummocks in water	early summer	sun	S or V
Meadow Lily	*Lilium canadense*	18"–30"	orange-yellow or reddish-yellow	on high mounds in boggy soil	midsummer	sun or light shade	S & B
★ Papyrus, Dwarf	*Cyperus haspan*	18"–24"	fanlike foliage, green	vertical accents by pools	summer	sun	V
Pickerelweed	*Pontederia*	24"–48"	lavender-blue	in clumps by ponds or bogs	summer	sun	V
Salvinia	*Salvinia*	Tiny, floating plants	green, inconspicuous	float on pool surfaces	summer	sun	V or spores
★ Siberian Iris	*Iris siberica*	24"–36"	blue, purple, white	on mounds in boggy locations	midsummer	sun	Rootstocks
Umbrella Plant	*Cyperus*	24"–48"	greenish-brown, prickly clusters	streamsides and other wetlands	late summer	sun	S
★ Water Lily, Hardy	*Nymphaea*	Blooms on water surface	white, yellow, red, pink	pools or large containers of water	summer	sun	R
Water Lily, Tropical	*Nymphaea*	Blooms on water surface	mostly blue and purple	pools or large water containers	summer	sun	R

FLOWERING VINES GROWN AS ANNUALS OR TENDER PERENNIALS

COMMON NAME	SCIENTIFIC NAME	APPROX. HEIGHT	RANGE OF COLORS	BEST USES	PEAK BLOOM SEASON	SUN OR SHADE	GROWN* FROM
Balsam Pear	*Mormodica charantia* (annual)	open vine	yellow, pear-shaped fruits	a curiosity, best planted in the background	summer	sun	S
Black-eyed Susan Vine	*Thunbergia alata* (annual)	short	orange or white with black center; short; light-green foliage	hanging baskets or trailing from a planter	late summer	sun	S
Canary Bird Vine	*Tropaeolum peregrinum* (annual)	4 to 6 ft.	small, fancy yellow blossoms; lobed leaves	hanging baskets or trailing over low fences	early summer	sun (not heat-resistant)	S
★ Cardinal Climber and Cypress Vine	*Quamlocit pinnata* (annual)	8 to 10 ft.	red, white; finely cut leaves	covering unsightly posts and walls; withstands dry winds	all summer	sun	S
★ Gourds, Ornamental	*Cucurbita species* (annual)	rampant, coarse	decorative fruit; odd shapes and colors; yellow, cream flowers	not pretty; place at rear of garden; give plenty of room	late summer	sun	S
Hyacinth Bean	*Dolichos lablab* (tender perennial)	8 to 10 ft.	small, pealike, purple to white blossoms; twining	attractive; use on fences at entryway	early summer	sun	S
★ Moonflower	*Calonyction aculeatum* (annual)	high climber	large, heart-shaped leaves; waxy-white blooms open at night	large containers; best at night	late summer	sun	S
★ Morning Glory	*Ipomea purpurea* (annual)	high climber	large mixed-color; blossoms at dawn	versatile vine for screening	all summer	sun	S
Passion Flower or Maypop	*Passiflora incarnata* (tender perennial)	spreading vine	Interesting purple and white flowers	cut flowers, edible fruit	early summer	sun	S
Rosa de Montana or Confederate Vine	*Antigonon leptopus* (tender perennial)	profuse growth	clusters of small, lavender, pea-shaped flowers; arrow-shaped leaves	covering porches & trellises	all summer	sun; heat resistant	S
★ Scarlet Runner Bean	*Phaseolus coccineus* (annual)	medium	vivid red & white bicolored flowers in clusters; dark-green foliage	children's gardens; fences of vegetable gardens; edible pods	midsummer	sun	S

*Legend: S=Seeds, V=Vegetative divisions.

8 ANNUALS: IMPORTANT KINDS DESCRIBED IN DETAIL

To make it easier to select annuals for your garden plan, this chapter will list important kinds of annuals by their class—either cool-weather annuals or summer annuals. Peak bloom seasons will be listed in order of importance:

Spring, beginning when days grow warm; about when deciduous fruit trees begin to bloom.

Summer, beginning when oak, walnut, or hickory trees have come into full leaf.

Fall, beginning with the first light frosts or fall rains.

Winter, beginning with the first snows in the north or in high-altitude areas, or when the leaves have fallen from deciduous trees in mild-winter areas.

The preference of the flower for sun or shade will be given; for instance, some flowers demand full sun because their blossoms close when shaded. Others grow in the sun in their native habitat and simply don't adapt to the cool dampness of shade. Most flowers don't seem to mind three or four hours of daily shade from a fence or wall, but only a few will grow in the medium to heavy shade cast by trees. In hot desert areas even summer annuals should be planted along the east or north side of the house or walls to give them respite from the blazing afternoon sun.

COOL-WEATHER ANNUALS

These are planted in the late summer or fall where winters are mild, in the early spring where winters are severe. The object is to schedule their planting so they bloom in cool weather, because hot weather makes them set seed and go out of bloom.

Cool-weather annuals generally perform best along the cool Western coastal belt; in the Far Southwest; in the Deep South (Gulf Coast climates where citrus can be grown); in the cool mountain and high desert areas; in the northern tier of states from Maine to Washington (and Canada and Alaska).

Cool-weather annuals generally are poorly adapted to the lower Midwest, the Midsouth, the Central and Southern Great Plains, and to the parts of the West where summer temperatures are high and winters severe.

AFRICAN DAISY OR CAPE MARIGOLD
Dimorphotheca sinuata (aurantiaca)

Robust plants with furry leaves. The most commonly planted species, *Dimorphotheca sinuata,* begins blooming at a height of 4–6 inches, but will reach 16 inches or more by late spring. Its flowers are 1–2 inches in diameter with contrasting centers; they close at night or in foggy or cloudy weather. 'Glistening White,' a variety of the *Dimorphotheca pluvialis* species, grows much lower and has larger flowers.

Visitors to the Far Southwest and Southern California see the African Daisy blooming in great, warm-colored masses in the dead of winter and decide to plant it back home. However, when springplanted where summers are moist and warm, it produces lush growth and few flowers. It likes mild, dry weather; seeds or seedlings planted in late summer produce flower buds prior to the onset of winter. In the northern states seeds may be started indoors in spring and transplanted when frost danger is past. Prefers full sun.

Best uses: bedding and naturalizing along fence rows and roadsides.

ALYSSUM, SWEET
Lobularia maritima

One of the easiest-to-grow annuals. Valued for naturalizing along roadsides, for very low edgings and rock gardens, and for covering bloomed-out bulb beds.

The sweet alyssums have gained in popularity rapidly in recent years, primarily due to the introduction of new colors such as lavender-pink 'Rosie O'Day,' 4-inch height and deep violet 'Royal Carpet,' 4 inches which augment the old-fashioned white alyssum. 'Carpet of Snow' is the finest low-growing white.

Intensely fragrant sweet alyssum quickly spreads into blankets of color so solid that little of the green of leaves shows through. It cascades over rocks and walls, fills cracks between flagstones, and reseeds abundantly, providing sturdy young plants to take over when older plants become rangy and seedy. In the West sweet alyssum has escaped from gardens to provide cool-weather color along road cuts and seaside cliffs.

Plant seeds in spring, fall, or winter. Seeds will sprout during warm spells and within four to six weeks grow into precocious little tufts of bloom. Transplants best when small.

BABY'S BREATH
Gypsophila elegans

Frothy baby's breath gives substance without mass. Flowering stems branch again and again; each threadlike stem is tipped with a minute white or pink flower with cupped petals. Individual flowers are pea-sized or smaller, but each plant has dozens, even hundreds, of them.

Baby's breath can't be counted on to add much to the color of a garden; you can practically see through the plants because their leaves are few, narrow, and widely spaced. It is grown almost exclusively for arrangements and drying. It is planted here and there among more colorful flowers so that the loss of a few plants cut for arrangements won't be noticed. Fast-growing baby's breath seeds can be scattered among slower-growing summer annuals. When you have removed the baby's breath, the summer annuals will grow together. Plant frequently—every two to three weeks—to maintain a steady supply for cutting.

Not frost hardy, not heat resistant, but well worth growing. Plant in full sun in spring or late summer. Grows 12–18 inches high.

BACHELOR'S BUTTON OR CORNFLOWER
Centaurea cyanus

Plants are erect, branching, and clothed with narrow, gray-green leaves. These make excellent bedding flowers for sunny beds. Keep seed heads pinched off to prolong blooming. A few plants can supply an abundance of long-stemmed blossoms for bouquets and boutonnieres. Color mixtures contain deep wine and maroon shades as well as the blue, white, and pink that are generally available separately.

Bachelor's buttons dry up in very hot weather; therefore, to get a long bloom season, it is necessary to sow

69

seeds outdoors from late summer through fall in mild-winter areas. In the north bachelor's buttons may be seeded in late fall or early spring; the little seedlings are quite winter hardy. Started plants are readily available.

Tall color mixtures grow to 18 inches; to 30 inches if planted early. 'Jubilee Gem,' a blue dwarf, and 'Snow Bell' (white) are only 12–16 inches high.

CALENDULA OR POT MARIGOLD
Calendula officinalis

Beloved in mild-winter areas, the calendulas are planted in late summer for color from fall through late spring. Large, warm-toned orange, yellow or gold blossoms add cheer to gardens during gray days and provide cut flowers even when frost has nipped other annuals. Plants remain compact during spring; blossoms frequently reach 3 to 4½ inches in diameter. However, when days grow long and sunny, plants stretch to knee height, and flower diameter decreases to 2 inches.

Where winters are severe, calendulas may be purchased as seedlings or grown from seeds planted in late spring in garden rows. The plants will bloom sporadically through midsummer, then will put on a big show of blossoms in late summer. Many gardeners in the lower Midwest and South delay planting until midsummer to get a fall show of large blossoms at chrysanthemum time.

Calendulas include such hot colors that they are customarily used in beds edged with good blending colors such as blue (try lobelia) or white (candytuft or sweet alyssum). For dramatic contrast, back up orange calendulas with tall, deep-purple stock. Calendulas prefer full sun and grow 12–24 inches high—except for the 8–12-inch dwarfs recently introduced from Japan.

CALIFORNIA POPPY
Eschscholzia californica
State Flower of California

Brilliant orange, gold, or yellow cup-shaped flowers on 12–18-inch silvery-green plants with lacy leaves. California poppies blanket hillsides and road cuts from Baja California to the state of Washington. Growing in solid patches or among meadow grasses, they bloom from the first warm days of spring until the hills turn dry and brown.

California poppies are best suited to large western gardens, where they can brighten fence rows or grow at random among fruit trees or along driveways. Once established by fall or winter seeding, poppies will self-seed for years; some plants live over as perennials. This persistence makes the California poppies less useful in most small, contemporary gardens except for spots that are too dry for other annuals. Plants are not harmed by crowding.

Further east, in cool upland areas and northern states, California poppies grow well as early-spring-seeded annuals in sunny beds. Plants grow low and stay neat except where summer rainfall is excessive.

The variety 'Extra Golden' has deep reddish-orange flowers. 'Mission Bells,' a color mixture, shows mostly double and semidouble flowers and has a wide range of colors and bicolors—white, cream, yellow, pink, and salmon—and is better suited to gardens than to naturalizing. California poppies are not related to true poppies such as the Shirley or Oriental species.

CALLIOPSIS OR ANNUAL COREOPSIS
Coreopsis tinctoria

An old-fashioned annual that is staging a comeback now that neat, dwarf varieties are available. Wiry, open plants have slender, smooth stems bearing individual, rather small, daisylike blossoms. Colors are earthy—yellow, gold, brown, and maroon — with fascinating ringed and bicolored variations. Gaillardia makes a good companion flower.

Calliopsis grows quickly and easily from its rather large seeds. It may be fall-seeded in mild climates and planted outdoors in early spring elsewhere. Young plants tolerate light frosts. Calliopsis self-sows, and has become established along many roadsides in the southern Great Plains, where in midsummer songbirds may be seen gleaning seeds from its dried heads.

The tall, double-flowered, mixed-color selection grows to 3 feet and is best for backgrounds. Dwarf edging varieties, 8–12 inches high, come in separate colors or mixtures. Calliopsis grows best in the full sun and prefers 6 to 12 inches of space between plants. The numerous seed heads must be occasionally sheared off to keep plants blooming. To encourage regrowth fertilize lightly and water after shearing.

CANDYTUFT
Iberis umbellata and *I. amara*

Soft, pastel colors; hundreds of tiny, closely spaced, umbrella-form blossom clusters and fast growth distinguish candytuft *(I. umbellata)*. Plants grow quickly from seeds planted outdoors in sunny beds in early spring; light frosts don't harm young seedlings. Dwarf, 8-inch varieties are used for edging, but are rather short-lived. The 12- to 15-inch standard color mixtures for bedding and cut flowers are more popular because plants can be sheared to encourage a second flush of blooms. Widely adapted.

Fragrant hyacinth-flowered or rocket-flowered candytuft (*I. amara*) differs from the Globe type. The strong, upright, 15-inch plants bear three to six or more rocket-shaped spikes of white flowers. Spaced 12 inches apart, the plants make an unforgettable late-spring-blooming edging. Plants are frost-tender, slow to bloom, and require a long, cool period to reach full size. Consequently, they are most popular in mild-winter areas of California where they are fall planted, and across the Southwest and Gulf Coast for very early spring planting.

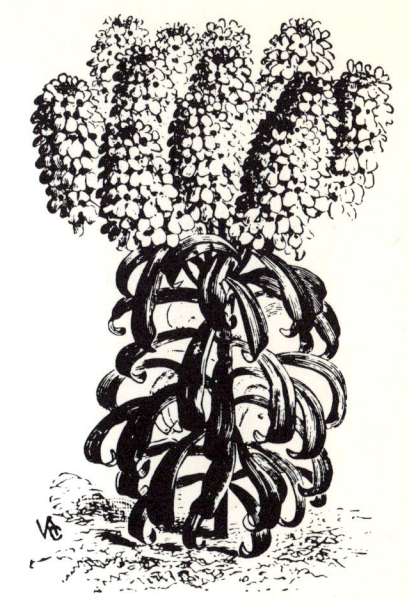

Iberis amara

Iberis umbellata

CLARKIA AND GODETIA
Godetia amoena and
G. unguiculata

These tall, cotton-candy-colored native flowers deserve greater popularity. Though botanically related and similar in their open, slender-branched, smooth-leaved plants, clarkia and godetia differ greatly in blossom form.

Godetia has satiny, single or semi-double cup-shaped flowers in lavender, pink, and white, tipped

71

Clarkia

with darker colors. Clarkia has more numerous flowers composed of doubled tufts of small, convoluted parts. The tall, mixed-color selections of both are excellent for cutting, but because of their informal, semiupright, 18–30 inch growth, they are best relegated to backgrounds, bulb-bed covers, etc. Dwarf varieties are available for edgings, but they bloom for only a short time.

Both clarkia and godetia make excellent early-spring-seeded flowers for all-summer bloom in mountain and northern states. In California and Arizona they are often fall-seeded with California poppies for naturalizing in dry, sunny meadows. To grow for cutting, space plants 12–18 inches apart to encourage branching. Whole branches may be taken for use as long-lasting spike flowers in arrangements.

DELPHINIUM, ANNUAL
Delphinium grandiflorum
(Chinese or Bouquet Delphinium)

Distinct from the tall, stately perennial type, "annual delphinium" is usually started anew from seeds each year. (Actually, it acts more like a biennial). One of the best blue flowers for cutting. Plants are 18–24 inches high, bushy and branching, often bearing six to twelve open spikes about 12 inches long. Individual flowers are 1 inch across. Separate blue colors include sky blue through gentian.

In mild-winter areas sow in late summer for bloom late the following spring (young plants are frost-hardy.). Elsewhere sow seeds outdoors in late fall. The young plants will live over and bloom the following summer. Plants need full sun and good drainage; they thrive in raised beds or sandy soil. Space delphiniums 2–3 feet apart to give them room to branch. They are not particularly easy to grow, but are worth the effort because the pure blue colors make beautiful cut flowers.

Other perennial forms of Delphinium such as the 'Pacific Giants' and 'Connecticut Yankees' are often treated as annuals in frost-free areas where perennials lack the desired winter dormancy.

LARKSPUR OR ANNUAL DELPHINIUM
Delphinium ajacis

Tall, columnar plants, best massed 12–18 inches apart in large beds. Leaves are finely cut; flowers come in long, slender spikes that are prized for cutting and drying. Shades in the many mixtures available include white, pink, lavender, blue, purple, and intergrades.

If Larkspur is to grow large and healthy and remain green through blossom time, its roots should be shaded from hot afternoon sun, either by adjacent bedding plants or by a 3-inch mulch of wood chips or straw. Where summers are cool, larkspur reaches 5 feet in height, but where hot summer follows on the heels of a short spring, plants grow only 18–24 inches and burn out in midsummer. Larkspur self-sows and naturalizes where drainage is good. Difficult to transplant except when seedlings are small. Sow seeds outdoors in late summer or fall in mild winter areas—in late fall or very early spring elsewhere. Sow thickly because seeds rarely germinate (sprout) strongly. Any one of the generally available double-flowered color mixtures is desirable. Seeds of separate colors are hard to find except in well-stocked packet seed displays.

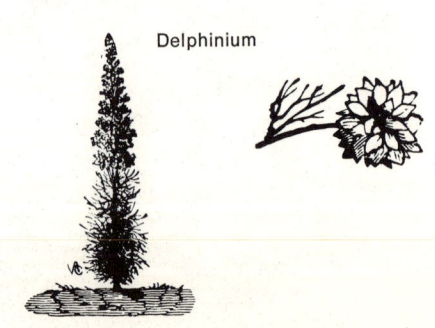

Delphinium

LOVE-IN-A-MIST OR DEVIL-IN-A-BUSH
Nigella damascena

This is a fast-blooming, easily grown flower with delightful light blue or pink blossoms. Each blossom is nestled in a cradle of slender, threadlike leaves—thus its quaint nicknames. After its petals drop, nigella forms curious, inflated, horned seed pods that may be dried for winter bouquets. Experienced gardeners keep a steady supply of blossoms coming for cut flowers by sowing small quantities of seed at three-week intervals.

New colors have been introduced: rose, purple, and white. While love-in-a-mist is too short-lived for use in display beds, seeds may be scattered among widely spaced plants of slower-growing summer annuals or among salad vegetables in the kitchen garden. The fluffy 12–24-inch plants may also be naturalized in informal borders.

NASTURTIUM
Tropaeolum majus

Among the top ten flowers in popularity, nasturtium serves many purposes. Sure-sprouting, fast-growing, nasturtium begins to blossom while plants are only saucepan size. The old saying that "nasturtiums do best in poor soil" is partially correct; actually, they do best in fairly dry soil protected from afternoon sun. Hot sun makes plants fade; moist, rich soil forces lush growth at the expense of flowers.

Nasturtium is frost-tender and dislikes hot weather. Yet, because of its rapid growth crops may be scheduled for both spring and fall bloom. Seeds ordinarily are planted outdoors because little is gained by indoor starting.

Varieties are grouped into two major classes; the 12–18-inch compact bedding types, and the "tall" or vining types. 'Jewel' mixed colors, a showy, compact, free-flowering variety, has many unusual shades and bears its flowers on long stems above the foliage. Of the compact separate colors, 'Cherry Rose' and 'Cherry Scarlet' share the long-sought habit of carrying their blossoms above the foliage. (Only the newer varieties or color mixtures have this desirable habit of bloom.)

Tall nasturtiums are mostly single-flowered; colors are in the yellow, orange, and maroon range, with many bicolors. The long vines can be trained up a trellis or allowed to trail over banks or walls. Nasturtiums have their share of pests, particularly aphids or plant lice. Fortunately, the new systemic insecticide sprays (see page 43) will eliminate them; scatter the granules down the sides of the row after seeds are planted.

NEMESIA
Nemesia strumosa

Small, mounded, 10–18-inch nemesia plants are covered with miniature, orchidlike blossoms in the brightest array of colors imaginable. Nemesia is so dazzling in large beds that it is customarily edged with cool blue violas or lobelias.

Nemesia is rarely seen outside of cool-summer areas. Frost-tender, it resents heat and dryness. Most gardeners start seeds very early indoors and transplant the seedlings into moist, fertile soil in order to enjoy the maximum span of bloom before hot weather blasts the plants. Nemesia is also suited to pot culture; pinch off tip growth to encourage bush growth.

English plantsmen have developed the best color mixtures. A dwarf 'Nana compacta' form is available.

Nemesia

NEMOPHILA OR BABY BLUE EYES
Nemophila menziesii

Quick-growing but short-lived, nemophila sets seeds and goes out of bloom with the onset of hot weather. The petite, 6–10-inch plants are used to cover bulb beds and to add spring color among shrubs. Cup-shaped flowers are sky blue with cream or white centers. A western native, it is best adapted to northern states and to the cooler areas of the West Coast.

Scatter seeds in sunny beds in early spring. May be fall or winter seeded in California and the Southwest.

PANSY AND VIOLA
Viola cornuta and
V. tricolor hortensis

Though technically perennials, pansies and violas are most often grown as annuals. In recent years they have been hybridized to such an extent that differences between the important varieties of the two species have been minimized. Pansies generally have large flowers with ornamental faces; violas have medium-sized, rounded flowers with clear colors and indistinct markings. Pansies are most often planted in mixed color beds; separate color violas are popular for edgings. Both grow 6–10 inches high at maturity. Pansies and violas are so inexpensive when purchased as blooming plants that few gardeners grow them from seeds except to get the unusual separate colors. Plants require 90 to 120 days from seeds to first bloom and are usually started indoors. However, good results may be obtained by late summer outdoor seeding in a protected bed, even in far-northern states. A light mulch, applied after the soil is frozen, minimizes loss due to the heaving of soil that alternately freezes and thaws.

No other plants can match pansies and violas for dependable winter and early spring color in mild-climate areas. Plants recover from fairly heavy frosts and quickly resume blooming. In hot areas pansies and violas are planted in light-to-moderate shade to prolong blooming. In cool-summer areas bloom will continue into the summer, but size will decrease as plants become rangy. Plants should be cut back and fertilized to encourage large blossoms; be sure to remove the seed pods in shearing.

Varieties and hybrids are numerous. The 'Swiss Giants' pansies are old favorites for winter bloom; the 'Majestic' hybrids are large-flowered and heat-resistant. Among violas, 'Clear Crystals' mixture has perhaps the best color range. Separate colors include clear blue, deep blue, purple, golden-yellow, ruby, white, and apricot.

Viola tricolor

PHLOX, ANNUAL
Phlox drummondi

Vivid colors, including most but true blue and orange, remind one of petunias, but phlox has erect, slender stems and bears its 1-inch-diameter flowers in overlapping clusters. Color mixtures are more often available than the separate colors (which include delicate shades of apricot and chamois as well as pink, red, and white). 'Beauty' and 'Globe' are among the best color mixtures.

Across East Texas and the lower South, where it is native, dazzling stands of the scarlet color phlox stop traffic. Yet, phlox is geographically adaptable, being one of the best flowers for early summer color in northern and eastern states. There are two distinct classes of phlox: the 12–18-inch bedding varieties and the 6–8-inch edging varieties. Starred and fringed types may be obtained, but they lack the color impact of the plain-blossom types. Don't confuse annual phlox with its tall perennial cousin, "summer phlox," a late bloomer.

Annual phlox tends to "bloom itself to death" in warm weather. If phlox is lightly sheared and fertilized when seeds begin to form, a second flush of flowers will soon follow. Annual phlox sprouts rapidly and blooms early when planted in early spring (seeds may even be scattered

Phlox drummondii cuspidata

Phlox drummondii, var. grandiflora

on snow-covered prepared beds); this peculiarity fits it for planting on daffodil beds and among early blooming shrubs to prolong the show of color. Perhaps the best use for annual phlox is to intersperse its plants among slow-growing summer annuals to gain extra weeks of color. Phlox plants are not invasive and are easy to transplant when small.

PINKS OR ANNUAL PINKS
Dianthus chinensis

Beloved by gardeners hundreds of years ago, pinks continue as a staple for edging and bedding. Blue-green plants with long, slender leaves produce blossoms over a long season, often over-wintering in the South and West. Long-stemmed plants with 1–2-inch blossoms arch gracefully for cutting.

"Pinks" are not all pink, but the color range is rather restricted. Scarlet, wine, mauve, lavender, rose, cream, white, and blush shades are often marked, zoned, edged, or eyed in contrasting shades. No two blossoms are alike in their fantastic array of frilled, fringed, ruffled, doubled, and twisted petal formations. Blossoms are smaller and less double than carnations, a first cousin of pinks.

Annual pinks are only slightly fragrant. Cut in the early morning and placed in a warm room, they breathe the faint, sweet scent of cloves. Cut flowers last for days.

Pinks are easy to start from seeds, either indoors or outdoors. Though happiest in moist, fairly fertile soil, they will survive long periods of dryness if seed pods are clipped off. Pinks are very hardy to frost. You can't go wrong with any of the color mixtures of pinks from seeds or started plants. Heights range from 8–24 inches. Some gardeners plant two or three seed packets, grow the plants until bloom color shows, and transplant similar shades into separate beds. Pinks transplant with no fuss if moved with a fairly generous root ball. 'Gaity' is a popular large-flowered color mixture that is showier than the very double 'Carnation Flowered' sorts. 'Bravo' is a good low-growing scarlet variety, and 'China Doll' is a recently introduced, showy color mixture with short, compact plants.

POPPY, ICELAND
Papaver nudicaule

Iceland poppies are perennials. Yet, because they are often grown as annuals, particularly in severe winter areas, they will be treated as such here. (In California and the Gulf Coast states Iceland poppies are grown as biennials or short-lived perennials.)

Iceland poppies have warm-colored, cup-shaped blossoms with petals like crumpled satin. Furry green buds nod on long, slender, leafless stems, gradually turning "sunny side up" as they split to unfold their tightly packed petals. Individual stems are fragile, but those knocked down by wind or rain are soon replaced by new growth.

Where winters are mild, Iceland poppies are started in late summer for late winter or early spring bloom. They transplant fairly easily if grown in peat pots and transplanted pot and all. Plants do not spread, and should be set on 8–10-inch centers. Because of their height and their warm colors, Iceland poppies are usually planted as bedding flowers and edged with agreeable companion flowers such as blue or yellow violas. Iceland poppy colors include yellow, orange, salmon, apricot, cream and white. 'Yellow wonder,' an All-America award-winner, has large, lemon-yellow blossoms on long stems.

Over much of the country, Iceland poppies should be started indoors in late winter and transplanted to the garden in midspring. Three to six weeks of bloom may be enjoyed before plants dry up from the heat. Plants with such a short bloom season are best employed in rock gardens or among shrubs so that when they cease blooming no conspicuous empty space will remain.

In far-northern states where heavy snow cover is the rule, Iceland poppies occasionally live over. Foliage dries and mostly disappears in late summer, leaving a sturdy root that can regrow early the following spring.

POPPY, SHIRLEY
Papaver rhoeas

Reserve this flower for informal beds where its unfailing return engagement will be welcome. Fat pods follow the 3-inch silken blossoms, spawning a prodigious crop of seeds that sprout early the following spring.

Shirley poppies were selected from the predominately red "Flanders Field" poppy that appears in the overgrazed pastures of Europe. Color mixtures contain deep red, scarlet, pink, rose, white, and apricot; some blossoms have contrasting centers, basal petal markings, or pencilled edges.

The fast-growing young plants are very frost-hardy, thus may be sown in fall or very early spring. Sow seeds where plants are to remain. Annual poppies may be killed or retarded in size and maturity if transplanted.

Placed in rather dry soil and full sun, Shirley poppies reach 18–36 inches, even more if crowded. The plants are rather rough and hairy looking and are best concealed behind lower-growing, dense bedding flowers such as pinks. Flowers may be cut for indoor use if taken just as they open. Exudation of milky juice from the cut stems may be stopped by touching the cut end to a hot burner or flame. Removing seed pods adds two or three weeks to the rather short bloom season.

"SCATTER GARDEN MIXTURES"

Mixtures of many kinds of flowers are sold under a number of names such as "Annual Flower Mixture" or "Cutflower Mixture." Certain seedsmen offer you the choice of "mixed tall flowers" or "mixed short flowers." These mixtures are to be preferred over those that have all sorts of flowers from 4 inches to 4 feet in height mixed together . . . for instance, when flower plants are wanted for specific purposes such as for cutting (tall) or rock gardens (short), you can purchase a mixture of seeds of flowers having the appropriate height. Read the description on the back of the packet to be sure you are buying the height you want.

Blends vary somewhat from season to season, even if purchased from the same seedsman. Reputable seed growers attempt to balance the proportion of ingredients to prevent any one kind from dominating the resulting planting. Generally, ten to twenty kinds are represented in a blend, including some odd and seldom-grown flowers.

Scatter garden mixtures usually include a preponderance of flowers that benefit from early spring planting. Early planting may result in the rotting of a few seeds of summer annuals such as zinnias in the blend, but the loss is hardly noticeable.

Mixtures delight children who like to watch for the strange new flowers as they mature. The beginning gardener should try a small planting of scatter garden mixtures even though friends who are experienced gardeners may make fun of them. Guessing the names of the many flowers and becoming acquainted with their colors and forms can be fun and can provide a big step toward deeper involvement with gardening.

OVERLEAF:
Bouquet of various bulbous plants

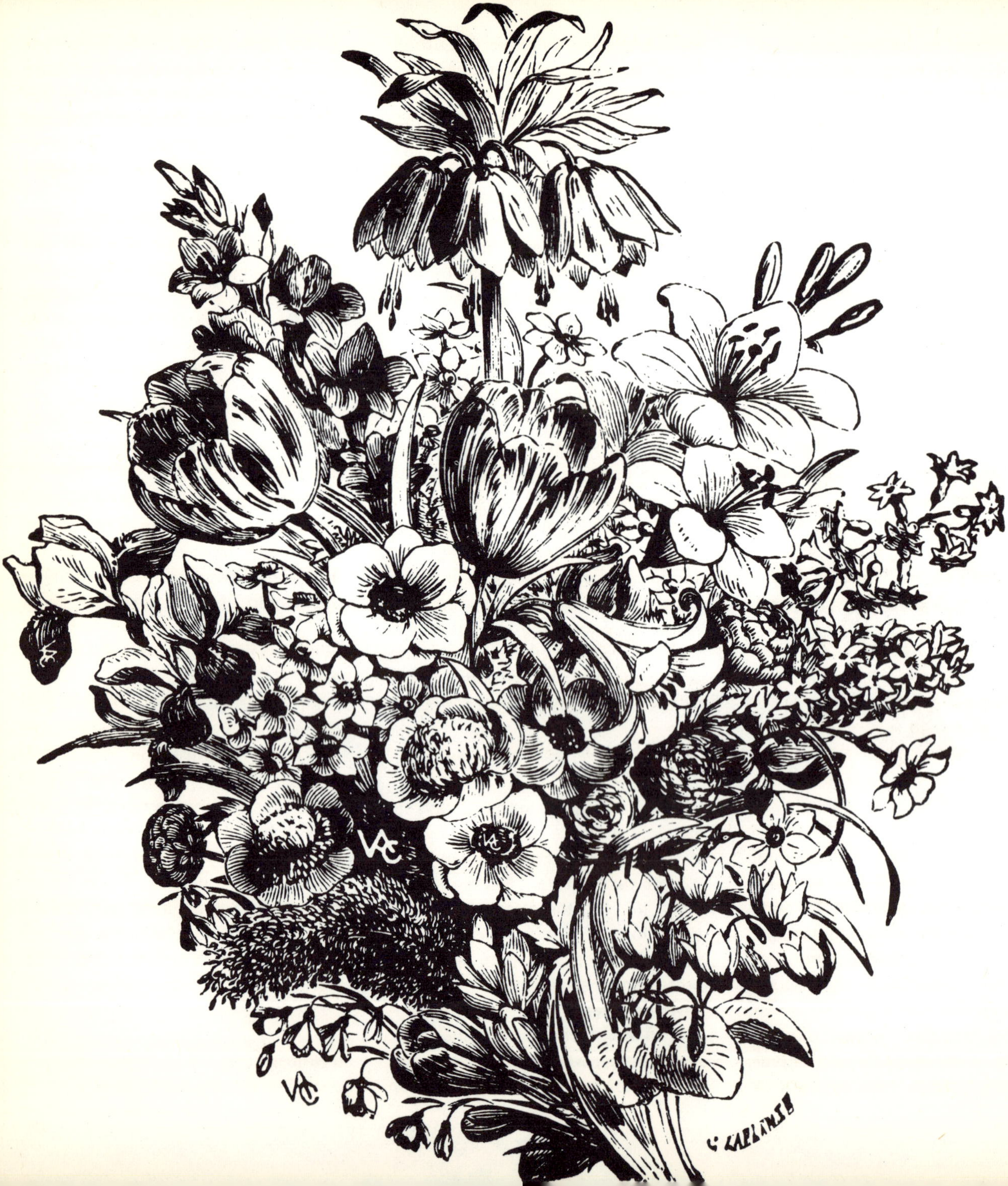

SNAPDRAGON
Antirrhinum majus

Much improved by plant breeders in recent years, modern snapdragons provide one of the best tall plants for vertical accents in the garden and massive spike flowers for cutting.

Garden snapdragons form basal branches if tops are pinched out when plants are 6–9 inches high. Base-branching produces more spikes and a bushier plant that is less likely to blow over. Even with pinching, western-grown plants usually require staking because the long, winter season allows plants to grow 3–4 feet high.

Snapdragons are usually purchased as plants or started indoors, because seeds are small and plants require eight to ten weeks to reach a size that can cope with weeds and inclement weather. Seedlings transplant easily. Early-planted snapdragons produce a longer period of bloom before the rust diseases arrive with hot, humid weather. Modern varieties resist rust for a few weeks, managing to grow in spite of its disfiguring ravages, but gradually rust gets the upper hand. Western and southern gardeners have learned to plant seeds in late summer for late winter and spring bloom, when rust poses no problems.

Among the best garden snapdragons are the 'Rocket' hybrids and the open-faced 'Bright Butterflies' and 'Madam Butterfly' hybrids.

Colors include most but true blue. Bicolors and gaudy "art shades" are available in the various 'Tetra' strains. Dwarf snapdragons—desirable for edging and rock gardens—can be found in some seed racks, and include 'Floral Carpet' and the recently introduced 'Little Darlin's' color mixtures. Both tall and short types respond well to shearing after the first blooms have dropped.

STOCK
Matthiola incana

Of greatest value for gardens where stock can provide an abundance of winter and spring color. In such mild-winter areas, late-summer planted stock forms good-sized plants and heavy flower spikes. In northern states stock should be started indoors in late winter and transplanted to the garden in late spring; or purchased as large seedlings for transplanting—the larger the better.

Stock is perhaps the most useful and satisfactory spike flower for cutting. Fragrant, long-lasting spikes are densely packed with blossoms. Their soft pastel pink, cream, rose, lavender, purple, and white shades blend in bouquets with peonies, iris, and lilacs.

Plant breeders have not been completely successful in eliminating the rather plain single-flowered plants from stock. Consequently, it is good practice to plant stock quite thickly so that it can be thinned when the single-flowered plants begin to show their distinctive spindly growth. Double-flowered plants are robust and stocky with thick stems.

Combine stock in sunny beds with pastel-colored edgings such as pinks or dwarf snaps. The 'Dwarf Ten Weeks' variety, a favorite in the East, is only 12–18 inches tall; its plants branch into bushy, spreading specimens, completely filling beds with color. The tall 'Giant' or 'Column' stock varieties (which do best in western states) reach 24–36 inches in height and have fewer branches.

SWEET PEA
Lathryus odorata

Few flowers are easier to arrange in

quaint, simple bouquets than long-stemmed sweet peas. The leafless, slightly curving stems are easy to gather; flowers last for days. Sweet peas are grown mostly on the West Coast, in New England, in the Mountain states, and in parts of Florida and south Texas where they live over winter. They are difficult to grow in the Midwest and Midsouth.

Sweet peas have fallen into disfavor in recent years because of the care required to train and tie the tall vines up fences, trellises, or netting. Now, however, dwarf and intermediate height varieties are available that need no strings or stakes and can be planted in open beds.

Sweet pea varieties are classified by blooming periods: winter to early spring; late spring to summer. The heat-resistant varieties developed for late-spring bloom will not flower on short, gloomy winter days; conversely, the winter-bloom varieties have little heat resistance and are of limited value for any areas outside of frost-free gardens in Florida and California.

The 'Royal Family,' 'Galaxy,' and 'Knee-Hi' classes are of the heat-resistant type and are customarily planted in early spring. Where winters are severe and summers are warm, start seeds early indoors in peat pots and set plants outdoors in late spring.

The winter-flowering types are planted outdoors in late summer where winters are mild, the object being to start them in time to get a good set of buds before cold, wet winter weather sets in. This is how some California gardeners manage to grow sweet pea blossoms for Christmas decorations. The dwarf 'Bijou' variety blossoms dependably during the winter.

'Knee-Hi' is becoming a popular spring-blooming variety. Its vines form mounds 18–30 inches high, requiring no strings or stakes. In rich soil it develops stems averaging 12–16 inches in length, a desirable size for bouquets. Each stem bears five to seven large, fragrant, ruffled blooms. The 'Americana' color series, recently introduced, is, similar to 'Knee-hi.'

Sweet peas come in separate colors and in mixtures of fifteen to twenty delicious pastel shades, all *except* yellow, orange, and true blue.

Lathyrus odorata

SUMMER ANNUALS

The important flowers singled out for detailed descriptions in this section have been selected from those with the best sales records of seeds and started plants. You will see that the rather robust, carefree flowers make up the majority of the list, particularly among summer annuals. The low-growing flowers have generally gained in popularity because contemporary homes and gardens are often too small for the bushy, invasive flowers that grow to shoulder height in a few weeks. Gardeners have also made their preference for prolonged bloom plainly known. The flash-in-the-pan flowers, no matter how lovely, never make the grade except among advanced amateurs who grow them occasionally out of sentiment or curiosity.

Resistance to heat and humidity. Particularly valued are the qualities of resistance to heat and humidity —the ability to continue to set blossoms when days are fiercely hot. Gardeners who live where summers are cool find it hard to believe that seemingly indestructible petunias, marigolds, and zinnias, can literally go to pieces during dog days in the South. Conversely, southern gardeners can't conceive of sweet peas blooming in July or of summers so cool that giant zinnias don't open until just before killing frost.

Get more mileage out of summer annuals. There are tricks to getting more mileage out of summer annuals. Across the South, where summer rains can be heavy, gardeners customarily build flower beds 6–12 inches above the lawn area. Then, when the heavy thundershowers come—the kind they call "toad stranglers"—the flowers don't perish from the root rot that can follow flooding. In the desert areas of the Southwest gardeners tuck flowerbeds under overhangs, behind walls, in the lee of cactus hedges—anywhere, in short, that they can receive some shelter from the hot afternoon sun.

It takes a while for emigrants from cooler climes to learn that in the South almost everyone "relaxes" for two or three months in midsummer. It is a sensible arrangement—what does it matter if the flower garden deteriorates while folks relax, they simply replant in August and enjoy an entirely fresh garden through the fall.

Actually, much more can be done to create favorable "microclimates" in cool-area gardens than where summers are hot. Gardeners in the northern tier of states, in high-altitude areas, and in cool seacoast towns can coax additional weeks of bloom from summer annuals by starting them early and by placing them in protected beds where reflected sun intensifies the warmth and where the heat stored in rocks or walks or walls radiates and warms the air on cool nights.

AMARANTHUS (JOSEPH'S COAT AND LOVE-LIES-BLEEDING)
A. tricolor and A. caudatus

"Joseph's coat" sprouts rapidly from seeds sown in warm garden soil. If you've never before seen this species of amaranthus, plant it in rows so you won't confuse it with weeds. Don't yank out plants because they still look drab green or bronze at a height of 3–4 feet—at about that stage the crown leaves begin to turn color. Then, as new leaves continue to develop, they, too, will sport wild variegations of yellow, green, cream, and maroon.

The variety 'Molten Fire' is a knockout, as are the early-flowering 'Early Splendor' and the willow-leaved 'Flaming Fountain.' The crown leaves are vivid, luminous crimson-cerise against the maroon lower foliage.

'Kiss-me-over-the-garden-gate' is perhaps a more apt name for *Amaranthus caudatus* than 'Love-lies-bleeding.' The tall plants were a feature around fences and gates in Victorian gardens during the era when many flowers gathered romantic nicknames. Long, chenille-like, pink fronds hang from the tips of branches.

All amaranthus species prefer full sun and rich soil. The heavy plants should be placed against a fence, where they can be tied up if knocked awry by a wind-storm.

Best use—as backgrounds "way back" in a corner of the garden.

Amaranthus caudatus

These plants are more curious than beautiful and are so dominant that they take the play away from more discreet flowers. Amaranthus can be cut for arrangements, but the cut ends of stems must be sealed with flame or with boiling water to prevent wilting.

ASTER OR CHINA ASTER
Calistephus chinensis

Asters are among the most popular of all flowers for cutting because of their long, slender, strong stems, and good keeping qualities. They are generally available in seed displays in a wide range of separate colors and complete color mixtures. Easy to grow.

Among all asters the 'Crego' types are the favorites, with their large blossoms of twisted petals. Many flower arrangers prefer the 'Powder-puffs' types with their more numer-

Aster

ous, slightly smaller blossoms that have rolled petals. Miscellaneous varieties include types with larger diameter blossoms having but a single row of petals. Most asters grow 12–36 inches high.

Rains get asters down. Their heavy blossoms droop, sometimes down to the ground. For this reason they are not often used in beds for close-up inspection. However, a recently introduced dwarf aster, 'Queen,' doesn't fall apart in the rain. Its short, stiff stems are not as useful for cutting—consequently dwarf 'Queen' is most often used for edgings. Asters are not particularly frost-resistant but prefer cool weather.

Asters are, unfortunately, occasionally affected by a virus disease called "yellows," thought to be carried by such insects as aphids and leafhoppers. The disease causes plants to turn greenish yellow and to die. There is no cure, but a regular program of spraying for insects offers fairly reliable control through prevention.

Best uses—cutting, low backgrounds, and, for dwarf 'Queen' asters, edging. Asters bloom in early summer in the South and West; later plantings bloom in the fall. Early fall is bloom time north of the Mason-Dixon line.

BALSAM OR TOUCH-ME-NOT
Impatiens balsaminea

Easy to grow and blooms quickly from seeds or started plants. The plants are brittle and the blossoms rather delicate, thus the common name.

Consider balsam for beds that are protected from the afternoon sun (except in cool-summer areas). Choose the tall type if you want knee-high plants that show blossoms at every joint of the main stem. Select the dwarf "camellia-flowered" types for greater color impact—these newer varieties carry their blossoms at the tip of each branch.

The colors of most varieties of balsam are pastel, like ice cream or sherbet. Newer varieties such as the dwarf 'Tom Thumb' include vivid scarlet and purple shades. You can float the blossoms or use them as filler flowers in arrangements.

Balsam is good for beginning gardeners because it is easy to grow and it blooms for months except where summers are quite hot. It isn't among the most popular summer annuals, probably because most balsam colors are muted. Personally, I like the relief that pastel balsam provides from the firecracker colors that are currently the rage.

Best uses—lightly shaded beds (doesn't require edging flowers), children's gardens.

BEGONIA, FIBROUS ROOTED OR WAX BEGONIA
Begonia semperflorens

Compact, mounted plants are literally smothered with clusters of small flowers. Every part of this flower looks freshly waxed. Recently introduced hybrids can withstand summer heat, but they need light shade in gardens south of the

Mason-Dixon line. In cool parts of California begonias bloom the year round in sheltered beds. Wax begonias are among the best edging flowers because the plants spread into a solid low hedge that does not fall apart in wind or rain. Individual plants in pots may be brought indoors for use as centerpieces.

Don't try to grow begonias from seeds unless you have a greenhouse; begonia seeds are fine as dust and slow-growing. Purchased plants begin blooming while still quite small. Good hybrid color mixtures and separate colors are available, such as 'Charm' and 'Thousand Wonders' begonias; all are soft and pleasing.

Best uses—edging, massed beds, containers, lightly shaded areas.

CELOSIA, PLUME CELOSIA AND COCKSCOMB
Celosia plumosa and *C. cristata*

Many fanciful names have been given the celosias—"Plume celosia" is descriptive, as is "Cockscomb" for *C. cristata*.

Feathery plume celosia comes in numerous sizes and colors. Most useful are the varieties with large plants whose heads can be harvested for arrangements and for drying. Hang the heads upside down in a warm, dry place; the dried colors will be very close to the original. Or, use the silica gel drying compounds; these soak up plant juices so efficiently that almost

Celosia

all the natural fresh color is retained. Separate red and gold shades are available; a most flamboyant scarlet is 'Forest Fire' with chocolaty-maroon foliage. A choice gold is 'Golden Triumph'; 'Golden Fleece' is chartreuse yellow. The dwarf plume celosias such as 'Meadow Glow' are rather spikey for edgings—they look best when massed in beds or grounded among drifts of white petunias. Groups of three to five plants look good when grown in roomy containers.

The cockscombs have a top-heavy appearance because of the massive, convoluted, damask-textured heads. Locate them in "cutting rows" at the rear of the garden. Fantastically colored dwarf varieties such as the 'Coral Garden' series are available

from Japan and Europe but are so short that they can suffer a pelting with mud from every rain or sprinkling unless mulch covers the soil. All celosias grow quickly from seeds sown in warm soil. In northern states started plants will give weeks of additional bloom. The All-America winner 'Fireglow,' a cardinal red, is widely available in plants and seeds. If you purchase plants, get them just when flowers are starting to form, or even earlier. Avoid the plants in full bloom in flats—these are often set back so completely by transplanting that they never resume active growth and development.

Best uses—cutting, drying, backgrounds, bedding.

COLEUS
Coleus blumei

Coleus is grown for its broad, varicolored, crinkled or rumpled leaves. No two plants are alike in markings or in the serrated leaf margins.

Coleus begins to "show its stripes" when plants are no bigger than a kitten's ears. You can look over the selection of started plants in pots at the nursery and choose ones that suit your fancy. Give coleus rich soil and plenty of water and it will grow 2 feet high. It may seem cruel to pinch out the tips of growing branches, but grit your teeth and do it. New branches will pop out along the lower stem, forming bushier plants.

The blue spike flowers on coleus are an extra added attraction, but some gardeners prefer to keep them neatly pinched off.

Coleus grown in full sun tends to fade to a dull greenish-brown. Conversely, plants grown in lightly shaded beds develop intense colors. You will doubtless become attracted to certain plants because of their novel colors; you can save them to enjoy the following summer by taking "tip cuttings." Just before fall frost, cut off the tips of stems to make "slips" about 6 inches long, and root them in soil or water. Keep them over winter as pot plants.

Color mixtures of coleus are generally available as seeds or plants; the separate shades are expensive but worth the extra cost.

Best uses—shaded beds or planters, pot plants.

COSMOS
Cosmos bipinnatus

There is a clean, wholesome exuberance about cosmos plants. They make themselves at home wherever you plant them, billowing out lacy branches to fill open spaces and to reach engagingly through fences. There is nothing prim or inhibited about cosmos, yet one never tires of them. I suppose it is because cosmos is neither bold nor angular —the foliage is altogether fluffy and mild-green, and the daisylike tufted flowers are in pastel shades.

Cosmos is often seen along farm fences, waxy buds glistening in the hot sun, blossoms flirting with every breeze. Cosmos is equally at home in city gardens, but give it room to grow. One plant can expand to the size of a small barrel.

Cosmos flowers last only a day but if you use the tips of branches in arrangements, new flowers will open over a period of several days.

Another cosmos with yellow or scarlet flowers is occasionally seen in seed racks. Its colors are hot and vivid; its plants, unfortunately, are somewhat coarse and rampant except where summers are short. These bright cosmos can make a vibrant contribution to a warm color scheme and supply lots of cut flowers. 'Sunset,' a vermilion color, is widely available.

Cosmos grows so readily from seeds that started plants are rarely offered. Plant in full sun.

Best uses—backgrounds, temporary shrubs.

FLOWERING TOBACCO
Nicotiana

This evening-opening flower can evoke memories. Nicotiana isn't much to look at but is it fragrant! Once you have experienced a garden scented on summer evenings by nicotiana, you can walk into a garden anywhere and know without looking that nicotiana is there, too. (Breeders have developed nicotiana varieties that remain open during daylight hours, but some of these varieties lack fragrance.)

Nicotiana has slender, upright plants with wide, furry leaves that diminish in size toward the top of the plant. Fully one half the plant is formed of open spikes of tubular flowers that are tipped down. The old-fashioned fragrant types are 2–3 feet high and have greenish white or lavender flowers. The newer varieties are shorter, open day and night, and have brighter colors.

Light shade doesn't faze nicotiana, nor does full summer sun except in the Deep South and Southwest. Seeds are small and slow to grow until the plants are the size of your hand, then they pop up like a jack-in-the-box.

Best uses—fragrance, bedding, in light shade.

FOUR O'CLOCK (MARVEL OF PERU)
Mirabilis jalapa

Don't expect four o'clocks to be punctual. Their tightly wrapped flower buds usually open when shadows are growing long, which can be at a late hour at the height of summer. Cloudy days can also trigger the buds to open at off-hours. But when the buds finally do open, what a sight! Hundreds of inch-wide tubular flowers per plant

'Little Darlin's' snapdragons. *Courtesy Goldsmith Seeds*

'Butterscotch' dwarf marigold. *Courtesy Ferry-Morse Seed Co.*

'Old Mexico' Mexican zinnia. *Courtesy Ferry-Morse Seed Co.*

—in bright colors that shine against the large, deep green, arrow-shaped leaves. The blossoms remain open all night and until midmorning.

This old-fashioned flower has made a comeback because it can exist despite urban fumes and grime. I have seen plants flourishing around the stoops of homes in the congested heart of big cities. The smooth leaves collect very little soot and are easily washed off by rain or sprinkling.

Four o'clock plants are big and solid. In the north they grow 2–3 feet high and equally as wide. Where winters are mild and the perennial root lives over, plants may reach 4 feet in height.

New plants "volunteer" from seeds dropped from the previous year's four o'clocks, but they won't show the same flower colors as the parent. In fact, four o'clocks may bear flowers of more than one color or pattern on the same plant—a fascinating freak of nature.

Place plants in full sun or light shade. Start the large, peppercorn-like seeds in warm soil outdoors; plants are hard to purchase. Four o'clocks grow very fast.

Best uses—temporary shrubs or hedges, childrens' gardens, city gardens—not good for cutting.

GERANIUM
Pelargonium hortorum

The recent advent of geraniums from seeds has brought this universally loved flower from the class of an expensive pot plant into the price range of bedding plants. Formerly grown only from cuttings and available at fancy prices as pot plants, geraniums can now be used lavishly in large beds of pink, white, or the unmistakable "geranium red."

Technically, geraniums are tender perennials and they do live over winter in parts of California. But elsewhere they are treated as summer annuals to be started indoors and transplanted as soon as frost danger is past. Cuttings may be taken in the fall if you wish to save choice colors; they will root quickly and easily for potting.

The newer hybrids such as 'Carefree' bloom fairly early and dependably. However, plants that are started indoors or purchased should be fairly large at transplanting (about 4–6 inches high), or they will not bloom until fall where summers are cool. (Geraniums are only moderately resistant to heat.)

Plant breeders will soon be introducing a wide selection of low-growing geraniums from seeds, mostly early-blooming, single-flowered or semi-double types that bear long-stemmed flowers in large, round clusters. When these advanced types are introduced, geraniums will almost surely join marigolds, zinnias, and petunias in the circle of the most popular flowers in America.

GLOBE AMARANTH, OR OLD-FASHIONED BACHELOR BUTTON
Gomphrena globosa

The "old-fashioned bachelor button" nickname is most prevalent in Texas, where this rawhide-tough, heat-resistant flower is a staple summer item. All across the South gardeners rely on it because it is virtually the only cutting flower that produces blooms in midsummer. Yet, if started early indoors in northern states, globe amaranth will bloom for one to two months in all except very cool areas. Grow in full sun.

Gomphrena globosa

Plants are solid, compact, rather furry. Flower stems are long, free of leaves, wiry. The generally available mixed color seeds produce flowers 2–3 feet high, but dwarfs are also available for edgings. Colors are rather restricted, with purple and off-white predominating. A dull gold color is also occasionally seen. The blossoms are the size of a thimble and are formed of many layers of papery petals. When dried, blossoms remain intact for years.

This flower is in no way related to the cornflower *Centaurea,* which is also known as "bachelor button", and is only distantly related to *Amaranthus*. It is one of the many species called "everlastings" or "strawflowers" because of their keeping qualities.

Best uses—cutting, drying, bedding, edging.

GLORIOSA DAISY
Rudbeckia "hybrid"

Only a decade ago this flower was unknown; then, an enterprising seedsman tried it, became convinced of its value, dubbed it with a catchy name, and watched it rocket to the top dozen in popularity. He wisely promoted it as an annual even though technically it is a short-lived perennial.

Gloriosa daisy will be with us for a long time because big yellow daisies are useful as well as pretty. The ray flowers on the single-flowered varieties are as big as a saucer, yet not massive. The blossoms of the double-flowered type are smaller but more solid—packed with layers of narrow petals. The single-flowered types have mostly "zoned" blossoms ringed with mahogany or maroon. The newest gloriosa daisy, 'Irish Eyes,' is sunshine bright.

Best uses: massed in sunny beds for brilliance and for cutting. The long-stemmed blossoms last for days. The tall, rough, rugged plants are no more civilized than their "brown-eyed Susan" country cousins, but who notices the plants? Very resistant to heat; they bloom in southwestern heat that knocks even zinnias and marigolds out of bloom.

IMPATIENS OR SULTANA
Impatiens sultanii or *I. holstii*

This is a leading flowering plant for shaded beds. Impatiens has a lot going for it—clean, glossy-green leaves; neat, tidy plants; jewel-bright, open-faced blossoms; a cheerful indifference to heat. Its only dislikes are cool, windy gardens and intense sunlight.

For many years the color spectrum of impatiens was restricted to orange-scarlet, white, and lavender-pink. Now, exotic shades of purple, coral, pink, and crimson have been added. Bunched together, the new colors are too much; try little groups of the bright shades in a bed of white impatiens. Flowers of the newer colors are borne on low-growing plants, 6–10 inches high. 'Elfin' and 'Shady Lady' are among the better new dwarfs.

You can "slip" impatiens as you do coleus, by cutting the tips of branches and rooting them in water or soil. In this way your favorites can be carried over the winter as house plants. Set the potted plants on your kitchen windowsills; they will bloom if they receive plenty of sunshine. Move the pots on very cold nights or pull the drapes; the cold that radiates through a windowpane can severely shock or kill tender plants.

Don't let the terminology of "tender perennial" on some packets of impatiens confuse you. The term is technically correct, but since impatiens freezes out in virtually every climate, it is best treated as an annual. Best uses—beddings or edgings in shaded locations, containers.

MARIGOLD, AFRICAN OR AMERICAN
Tagetes erecta; named hybrids

Few people are neutral about marigolds; most praise them for their honest pungence and bravura colors, but some gardeners avoid them for the same reasons. I happen to like marigolds because a few plants of the tall type can reward you with armloads of long-stemmed blossoms. The big, husky plants seem to thrive on heavy pruning.

Plant breeders have done wonders with the giant-flowered marigolds that belong in this class. Now there are hybrids that bloom early and continuously in a multitude of blossom forms; hybrids that bloom when only knee high and others

Tagetes patula

that reach waist height before bursting out in full color.

If you are planting large beds of mixed-color marigolds, purchase seeds of the ordinary inexpensive mixtures; they are uniformly good. For separate colors, however, purchase the F_1 hybrids; their seeds or plants are more expensive, but they will produce uniform plants, all with the same height and blossom characteristics.

If you have always purchased plants for your garden, try seeds of giant-flowered marigolds. Plant them in sun-warmed soil in early summer and watch them shoot up. Marigolds are one of the most dependable flowers for "growing your own."

Plant in full sun. The hybrid 'Gold Coin' series comes in several colors, as does 'Climax' and 'Jubilee'.

MARIGOLD, FRENCH
Tagetes patula and named hybrids

Fifteen years ago, dwarf double-flowered French marigolds were the most popular *bedding* flower grown from seeds sown outdoors. Now, since hybridization has whittled down their height from 12 inches to 6 inches, they are the most popular *edging* flower. But don't assume that all dwarf double marigolds are the tiny tykes; plants of some older varieties still to be found in seed racks can grow big enough to fill a water bucket.

The midget strains and hybrids are uniform in size and growth habit; this is most important in edging flowers. You wouldn't like the looks of edging flowers humping up and down like an ill-assorted guard.

You can select from a number of colors and blossom forms. Some blossoms have a dark ruffle around a contrasting center crest or tuft. Others are solid shades—the light, clear yellow is better for combining with other colors than the rather contentious orange shades. The 'Nugget' series of colors is good, as are the 'Petites' and 'First Lady,' an 18–inch-high, light-yellow double-flowered hybrid.

Some gardeners grow the old-fashioned "single-flowered French marigolds" such as 'Dainty Marietta' for bedding. They have dollar-sized, daisy-flowered blossoms that bloom like crazy. The plants are rather large—16–18 inches high—too robust for edgings.

Marigolds grow rapidly from seeds sown in early summer in full sun and moistened twice daily by sprinkling, or you can purchase from a wide choice of started plants. If you are careful in transplanting, marigolds don't even seem to notice that they have been moved.

Children love these precocious little flowers that bloom when no larger than a teacup. Too, marigolds are durable enough to come back after rough treatment. Teachers often use marigold seeds for planting indoors in plastic cups or eggshell halves. After 8–10 weeks on a sunny windowsill the little plants can be taken home to individual gardens.

Best uses—edging, low bedding. Stems are too short to cut for any but small arrangements and for filler flowers.

MADAGASCAR PERIWINKLE
(Vinca or *Vinca rosea)*
Catharanthus rosea

Like impatiens, Madagascar periwinkle is a tender perennial grown almost entirely as an annual. It is unfortunate that the name "vinca" became associated with this plant because it is often confused with *Vinca minor,* a blue-flowered groundcover vine. Madagascar periwinkle will weather the confusion and continue to gain in popularity, you may be sure. It ranks with globe amaranth as a "must" for hot gardens, be they humid or bone dry from desert air. The leaves remain dark green and glossy (if plants are fed occasionally), and bloom set continues through 100-degree-plus weather.

Plants of the newer dwarf varieties range in height from 6–12 inches. The flower colors are clear, though limited to only a few shades. The older 2–3-feet varieties often have dingy colors. Plants grow slowly from seeds except from summer sowings out of doors in the South and Southwest. Northern gardeners are better off buying plants to get earlier bloom and a choice of blossom colors. 'Bright Eyes' or 'Polka Dot,' which are white varieties with a red dot in the center of the blossom, are beautiful when massed in large beds. 'Little Blanche' is pure white; 'Little Delicata' is delicate pink.

Best uses—edging, bedding, pots or planters in full sun. Not for cool windy areas. Stems can be cut; flowers last fairly well.

Petunia

PETUNIA
Petunia hybrida

Hundreds of thousands of dollars have been spent on the hybridization of petunias to produce more compact, lower-growing, disease-resistant plants with more and larger blossoms of brighter and more varied colors. That the effort has been worth the expenditure is attested by the status of petunias among garden flowers grown from seeds—first place! Largely because of sales of started plants in flats, market packs, and pots, petunias outrank even zinnias and marigolds.

Fortunately, the great variation in growth habits, blossom sizes, shapes, and colors saves petunias from becoming commonplace. Gardeners spread petunias around in great swatches of color because they can afford to paint with broad strokes—plants of most petunias are not expensive. I suggest, however, that you not take the line of least resistance and plant your entire garden with petunias. Instead, use them to hide the open soil around evergreens or background flowers, and to back up low edgings of other species.

Certain kinds of petunias were developed for use in large containers and hanging baskets. 'Cascade' hybrids, for example, have large plants with long stems that billow attractively.

In late summer, when your petunias begin to look ratty, take the shears to them and give them a severe cliping. Then, be kind and give them a good drink of water containing a moderate application of dissolved plant food. The plants will sprout new branches and recover to flower again in only a week or two.

Experiment with combining different petunia colors: peach, coral, lavender, and silver blue. You'll find them a welcome change from the ubiquitous red and white duet. If you like the bicolored blossoms—splashed, starred, or zoned with contrasting colors—use just a few in groupings and set them off with drifts of solid colors.

When you buy plants of petunias, get them on the young side, when colors are just beginning to show. Nip off the tips of long stems before planting. If the plants are tall and wiry (the growers call them "hard"), they will be slow to regrow when you transplant them to your garden. The hybrids of the "grandiflora" type have large blossoms, many with ruffled or wavy-edged petals. The "multifloras" have medium-sized, plain-edged blossoms. The double multifloras such as 'Cherry Tart,' 'Empress,' and 'Double Delight' are popular. You can't go wrong with the hybrids now on the market; just choose the color and blossom form that suits you.

Best uses — bedding, edging, among evergreen, hanging baskets and pots (use the fancy large-flowered types), and for cutting. You can cut whole branches without harming healthy petunia plants.

SALVIA OR SCARLET SAGE
Salvia splendens and
S. farinacae (Blue Salvia)

The red salvias, called Scarlet Sage, are perhaps the most evident flowers of all in late summer. Their color practically shouts at you from a city block away. And therein lies the problem. Most gardeners plant salvia in beds of one to two dozen plants or among evergreens, often in the front yard or near the street where the repetition from yard to yard can become monotonous, if not overpowering. How much more pleasing to the eye would be small groups of salvia set off by gray foliage plants such as dusty miller or by cream-colored zinnias.

Take a look around your neighborhood this summer, and if red salvia is too much in evidence, simply plan your salvia bed for the back yard. There you can enjoy it while your neighbors are treated to a new and different flower in your front yard.

Red salvia comes in a range of sizes, from less than a foot high for edgings to three feet in height for backgrounds. Occasionally you can buy plants of pink or purple salvia, or the beautiful silver-blue cousin, "Blue Bedder," *Salvia farinacae.*

Salvia can be grown from seeds sown outdoors, but it blooms late. Plants are more popular, purchased or started indoors 10–12 weeks prior to transplanting time. Salvia needs full sun and is killed by light frost.

Best uses — edging, bedding, background depending on height.

Salvia farinacae is especially good for cutting; its slender spikes are prized by flower arrangers. Some of the newer colors of *Salvia splendens,* such as 'Strawberry Sundae,' also look good in arrangements.

Salvia farinacea

SUNFLOWER
Helianthus annuus

Plant breeders have changed sunflowers so that you would hardly associate the beautiful new garden varieties with the old tall, large-flowered types. Most of the garden varieties have large but manageable plants that can be used as hedges, tall backgrounds, or temporary shrubs.

'Red and Gold' has 6-foot plants that bloom from midsummer through fall. The blossoms are single and in shades of red in combination with golden yellow. 'Sungold' is 5 feet high and has fully double flowers in a warm golden-yellow color. A dwarf form of this variety grows to only 18 inches in height. 'Teddy Bear,' uniform in height, grows 3 feet tall

Helianthus

—a useful size for backing up other summer annuals such as yellow zinnias and marigolds. The bright yellow flowers resemble 'mums.

There are few places in the garden for the old-fashioned tall or 'Mammoth' sunflower. Children love to grow them, and the plump seeds in the drying flower heads attract birds, especially jays and cardinals. The 10–15 feet plants are best placed in an out-of-way corner where they will not rob other garden plants of water and plant nutrients.

Best uses (garden varieties)—hedges, backgrounds, and temporary shrubs, wild bird plant.

Tall varieties—children's gardens.

VERBENA
Verbena hybrida

Verbena colors ring as sharp and

Verbena hybrida

clear as a bell. Individual flowers are small but closely clustered. The clusters spread to cover the plants, and the low-growing plants spread to cover flower beds. The result is corner-to-corner color in smashing reds, blues, pinks, purple, and stark white. Newer colors include amethyst shades and bicolors of white and red, white and blue.

Verbenas laugh at heat, yet bloom reliably in northern gardens from started plants. They are easy to grow except for one pest, a little grub called a "leaf miner" that tunnels inside the thick leaves and disfigures them. Use precautionary sprays or dusts of a residual insecticide every two weeks or an application of systemic insecticide. Verbenas are well worth the slight extra care.

Best uses—unsurpassed for planting in full sun in containers or raised planters where they can trail, or in drifts of separate colors among taller summer flowers such as marigolds or zinnias. Not good for cutting; flowers and leaves quickly wilt, even in water.

ZINNIA *Zinnia elegans*

Zinnias have come a long way from the scruffy native flower with "Mexican hat" blossoms that inhabits hillsides in Mexico and Central America. Now you can choose plants that range in height from 6 inches to 3 feet and select blossoms as small as a grape or as large as a dinner plate. The colors of zinnia blossoms differ in quality from most other flowers; most zinnia colors are strong and solid—almost heavy—when compared to the clean brilliance of verbenas, for example. Yet, there are luminous pastel pink and lavender shades in zinnias that are a delight to the flower arranger.

All zinnias are easy to grow from seeds started in full sun in warm garden soil. Nothing is gained by starting seeds early indoors or from rushing the season by planting seeds outdoors before the soil is warm. Zinnias transplant easily if moved while plants are small.

LARGE-FLOWERED ZINNIAS
18–30 inches in height

Always grow this kind from seeds. Purchased plants are usually too large for transplanting without severe shock. You can get seeds of varieties with plain or slightly cupped petals (dahlia flowered) or with twisted or rolled petals. Large seed displays may offer upwards of a dozen separate colors and bicolors of large flowered sorts as well as high-quality color mixtures. Some of the newer hybrids such as 'Zenith' have huge blossoms. The 'State Fair' color mixture contains many unusual shades.

Best uses—massed in beds or used in drifts as a background flower. Cut blossoms make long-lasting, bold arrangements in large containers.

SMALL-FLOWERED TALL ZINNIAS
18–30 inches in height

Some flower arrangers like this class because the stems are pliant and the blossoms are of a more versatile size. This class includes the 'Lilliput' and 'cut-and-come-again' varieties and color mixtures. You can get more color from these than from the large-flowered zinnias because although the flowers are smaller, they are also much more numerous. Try some of the delicate apricot, salmon, lavender, or cream shades.

Best uses—backgrounds, or for cutting.

DWARF ZINNIAS
8–12 inches in height

Try these little ones for edgings; the 'Thumbelina' zinnias grow only 8 inches high; the 'Tom Thumb' types to 12 inches. The diminutive blossoms can be used in miniature arrangements in demitasse cups, bud vases, etc.

Best uses—edgings, or in drifts among other small summer flowers such as dwarf gomphrena or 'Petite' Marigolds.

MISCELLANEOUS ZINNIAS
12–18 inches in height

The variegated 'Mexican' and 'Persian Carpet' zinnias and the orange *zinnis linearis* have medium-sized plants with long-stemmed blossoms. The leaves of these three are long, narrow, and slightly rolled, allowing the plants to get by on less moisture. Plant in hot, dry beds to keep them happy.

Best uses—Bedding and containers in dry locations. Excellent for cutting.

Lilliput Zinnia

9 PERENNIALS AND BIENNIALS: IMPORTANT KINDS DESCRIBED IN DETAIL

The work of improving perennials and biennials is proceeding more slowly than the breeding of annuals. Relatively few breeders in North America are concentrating on perennials and biennials because the economics of marketing do not encourage it. Consequently, many of the new introductions come from dedicated hobbyists and from northern Europe, where the cool climate favors the longer-lived plants. The plant societies have also made a great contribution to horticulture by encouraging their members to develop and introduce improved cultivars.

Where and when to buy plants. Perennials and biennials are most often sold as started plants grown from cuttings or other vegetative divisions. Some are sold as roots, bulbs or rhizomes ready to plant. This restricts the market largely to mail order and to a very short retail-store season in the late fall or early spring, when the young plants are dormant, yet not sprouting. Certain specialty nurserymen grow or sell perennials or biennials in pots or cans so that the customer can see the blooms before he buys the plant. This practice is particularly prevalent on the West Coast and across the South, where perennials never go fully dormant.

Growing from seeds. The only way to get many of the unusual perennials and biennials for your garden is to grow them from seeds. Fortunately, most of them are as easy to grow as the common annuals. You have to plan ahead, however, because you can't count on perennials and biennials to bloom the same season that you sow the seeds.

Certain Western and Southwestern states impose rigid controls on mail-order plants and roots from out-of-state. By the time the plants have endured several days of delays due to inspections, they are often weak or dead. For this reason many western gardeners grow most of their plants from seeds. State seed and nursery stock inspectors in many states have the legal right to open packages of seeds and plants addressed to you. But this is for your protection. It provides another quality control check to assure you of clean, healthy plants or seeds, free from harmful insects, diseases or contaminants.

Mark your plants with stakes. Plants of many perennials wither and disappear in late summer or fall. Mark them with stakes instead of relying on your memory to remind you not to dig in certain locations. Many kinds of plant labels are available —these mark the locations of plants and provide a permanent record of the kind and variety name.

ASTER, NEW ENGLAND & NEW YORK (MICHAELMAS DAISY)
Aster novi-belgii and *Aster novae-angliae* hybrids
Perennial

The value of fall or Indian summer flower color should not be overlooked. Often as much as a month of bloom can be enjoyed from perennial asters after most summer annuals are past their prime. Fall-blooming perennial asters are at their best in September and October, yielding long-stemmed clusters of daisy-like blossoms that combine well with fall foliage.

The older varieties of New England asters have long been used for fall-flowering backgrounds. Their tall, open plants are covered with hundreds of dime-sized blossoms until heavy frosts cut them down. However, their bushy growth restricts their use to sizable gardens and informal plantings along lanes and meadows or among large fieldstones. The native New York aster is similar to but only half the height of the New England species.

The English hybridized our native asters and produced what they call Michaelmas daisies, since they are in bloom in England at the Michaelmas season. From these crosses, many excellent early-blooming cultivars of more manageable height have been selected. Western breeders have produced hybrids that include their local species, some of which bloom in the summer on the Pacific coastal slope.

The choice of perennial asters is great, and the difference between certain cultivars is not enough for an amateur to discern. Visit display gardens in the early fall after phoning or writing for the date which their asters are expected to be in bloom. (Hardy garden chrysanthemums should also be in bloom at

Aster Novae-Angliae

the same time, so you can kill two birds with one stone.) You can find out from the superentindents at the display gardens where they purchase their plants. This is the only practical way to plan your fall garden.

Best uses—fall color in beds or backgrounds; cutting and drying.

BALLOON FLOWER
Platycodon grandiflorum
Perennial

Gardeners value the long-lived plants of balloon flower for good reasons. The steel blue of the flowers is a rare and beautiful color, and the buds are fun to watch as they slowly inflate and then open suddenly, and with an audible pop, by splitting into segments.

Plants are upright, 1–2 feet tall, and slender, branching into two or three stems. They look best when planted in groups of three to five among white or pink summer annuals or as a complement to pink phlox. They withstand light shade, but prefer full sun in all except desert areas.

White and pink-flowered varieties are available, but they are not as common as the blue. Plants are slow to become established in the North.

Best uses—blue color accents or focal points; cutting.

BLANKET FLOWER
Gaillardia garden hybrids
Perennial

Blanket flower shows its wild blood by enduring for years around old homesites and cemeteries and along roadsides. The 2–3-feet high

95

gray-green clumps spread to considerable size, but aren't invasive.

Plant breeders have given blanket flower much larger blossoms than its wild southwestern ancestor. Bands or rings of orange and maroon mark the yellow-daisy-like, long-stemmed blossoms, depending on the variety chosen. Blooms are abundant, midsummer to fall frost.

Blanket flower will withstand heat and drought. In humid areas blanket flower will last longer if planted in elevated sandy or gravelly mounds for good drainage. It grows easily and comes fairly true from seeds. The variations that occur are interesting and may please you more than the plants that are true to the variety you purchased. However, the only way to get the beautiful new 8-inch dwarf 'Sun Dance' is by ordering plants.

Best uses—summer color in hot, dry areas; covering dry, sandy hillocks; cutting.

BLEEDING HEART
Dicentra species.
Perennial

A long-lived flower for underplanting in dappled shade among trees or shrubs. Bleeding heart comes up early and does most of its growing before the trees are in full leaf. Western bleeding heart and fringed bleeding heart are low growing and combine beautifully with other woodland species such as ferns, bishop's hat, and trillium. All bleeding hearts have finely cut, delicate foliage.

Bleeding heart blooms at daffodil time. The common, or "Japanese," species, *Dicentra spectabilis*, yields long sprays of cutting flowers and is commonly planted with spring bulbs. In northern and northwestern states bloom continues sporadically through the summer. Newer cultivars of bleeding hearts such as 'Bountiful' bloom until fall frost.

Best uses—woodland underplanting, among shrubs, rock gardens, cutting. Not suited for mass plantings or edgings.

BUGLE OR BUGLE-WEED
Ajuga species and cultivars
Perennial

One of the most popular low-growing groundcover perennials in the U.S.A., bugle grows easily, spreads rapidly, yet is not difficult to keep within bounds. You can choose cultivars with either deep green, bronze, or cream-and-green variegated foliage. All have attractive short spikes of blue or pink flowers that are especially plentiful in cool weather. In the western states you can buy giant ajugas with larger leaves and taller plants than the common bugle.

Bugle carpets the ground so thickly that most summer weeds are choked out. However, it should be planted only in well-drained areas. Every few years bugle needs to be thinned in early spring, top-dressed with a mixture of moist peat moss and sand, and fertilized.

Plant bugle in the spring over most of the country; in the fall where winters are mild. It prefers light shade and will even establish itself under trees if given plenty of water.

Best uses—groundcover to fill in among shrubs and flagstones and to keep small corners of earth free from weeds.

CANTERBURY BELLS
Campanula medium
Biennial

Each plant becomes a veritable bell-tower of blossoms when the flower clusters open all along the knee-high to waist-high stems. Individual flowers are upright and as large as an egg cup. A small clump of Canterbury bells is quite a sight in late spring or early summer.

The plants decline rapidly after blooming and will dry up by midsummer. Allow seeds to scatter and sprout; strong new seedlings will live over the winter to blossom the following season . . . in early fall transplant those seedlings that are too close together.

Canterbury bells grow quickly and easily from seeds. In northern areas seedlings will survive the winter better if given a rough covering of dried cornstalks or evergreen branches after the ground has frozen. Remove the cover a bit at a time as the ground begins to thaw. No cover is needed where winters are short.

Best uses—backgrounds, mixed among later blooming perennials that will fill in the empty spots after Canterbury bells have dried up.

CHRYSANTHEMUM
Chrysanthemum moriflorum
Perennial, short-lived

The general run of florist's chrysanthemums are not reliably hardy across the northern half of the country, and many cultivars bloom so late out of doors as to be virtually useless. For this reason you should not waste your time trying to save gift plants of mums after they have bloomed, except where winters are mild.

Chrysanthemums do not come true from seeds, but the variety of color and blossom types from seeds is an asset. Small plants of hardy cultivars grown from cuttings are available in early spring by mail order and from local retailers. You can select from dozens of colors and blossom forms, most of them somewhat smaller than those from the florist shop. Occasional pinching of the tips of branches during the summer helps to make plants bushier. Discontinue pinching when buds begin to form. An alternative to pinching is the use of the new chemical sprays that keep chrysanthemums low-growing and bushy. Mums are voracious feeders but, paradoxically, are injured by slight excesses of chemical fertilizers.

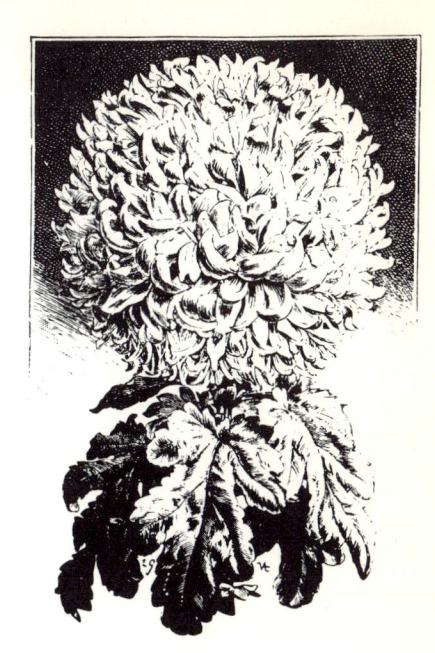

When fall frost has ruined the plants of mums, cut them back to a few inches above the ground unless you live in the North. There, leave the foliage to protect the crowns against freezing. Early the following spring dig up the plants and separate each into four to six divisions, discarding the woody center section. Replant the divisions, spacing them about 2 feet apart, or leave the mother plant in place and remove the green basal sprouts with roots attached, from around the outer perimeter of the old plants.

Fancy, large-flowered mums look best in display beds or containers, the early-blooming "cushion mums" make excellent informal companions to summer annuals. The low-growing, fall blooming cultivars prolong the bloom season of perennial beds and borders.

Best uses—display beds, containers, perennial borders, cutting.

COLUMBINE
Aquilegia hybrids and named cultivars

"Are they real?" people ask when they first see the fantastic blossoms of columbine. Some have unbelievably long, fragile spurs on birdlike blossoms. Other have shorter spurs twisted like horns. Yet others, called "clematiflora" for their resemblance to clematis blossoms, have no spurs at all.

Columbines are planted frequently, thanks to the general availability of good color mixtures of seeds and plants. Plants grow easily from summer-sown seeds and bloom the following spring. It is common for plants of columbine to live five to ten years in a well-drained site. The plants of columbine are neat and clean, worthy of placing at the most visible points in your garden. The long-stemmed blooms appear over an extended period beginning in the late spring, and may be cut for arrangements without harming the appearance of the plant. The plants are upright and of medium height; they look best in small groups where the variety of colors and blossom forms display to best advantage.

Best uses—among shrubs or boulders in rock gardens, or grouped as focal points among lower-growing summer annuals.

CORAL BELLS
Heuchera
Perennial

Few other perennials can match the prolonged bloom of coral bells. For week after week the low plants shoot up dozens of tall, wiry, leafless spikes topped by pale-pink, rose, coral-pink, chartreuse, white or red blossoms. The rosettes of foliage always look neat and fresh. Coral bells can be grown from seeds or plants.

You can see species of coral bells in gardens over most of the U.S.A. Many older homes in the Pacific Northwest and the Northeast have approach-walks lined with coral bells. Often, the plants have been there as long as the occupants, asking no more of them than an occasional thinning, watering, and feeding.

Best uses — edgings, among shrubs, among taller perennials, and for cutting. Coral bells are also a "natural" for rock gardens and the edges of woodlands; native plants can be found in just such locales. Hummingbirds are attracted to the flower spikes.

DAYLILY
(SEE HEMEROCALLIS)

DELPHINIUM
Delphinium hybrids
Perennial

You can stage a "Hollywood Spectacular" in your own garden with just one well-grown plant of delphinium. The heavy spikes are as long as your arm and can reach 3–5 feet in height. Each 1–2-inch flower on the spike is a study in iridescence, with overlays of hues that change as you walk around the plant.

Think twice before you shoehorn a shimmering, starlike delphinium into a bed of other perennials. Find a corner away from the wind for delphiniums where you can enjoy them as a unique creation. Or, intersperse them among summer-blooming hybrid lilies.

Delphiniums bloom in early summer. The flower spikes should be cut to near ground level soon after the last flower on the spike has faded. Fertilize and water the plants well, and you can expect a second set of blooms in late summer. A good plant can be propagated from cuttings.

Best uses—Special beds, cutting. The blues and purples are the best shades, the white is pure; the pinks are a little on the lavender side, but improvement goes on.

FORGET-ME-NOT
Myosotis sylvatica and
M. scorpiodes
Perennial

Indeed, you can't forget this flower; it won't let you. Forget-me-not usually comes back each year, from either roots or volunteer seedlings. Yet the plants rarely intrude where they aren't wanted—they stay within the high shade cast by trees or large shrubs; in moist, woodsy glens or along streambeds they carpet the ground with a blue blanket.

The easy-to-grow plants of forget-me-not are small and dainty, as are the blossoms. Some seed mixtures contain flowers with pink or yellow centers. Plants stay in bloom during most of the summer in the North and during spring and fall where summers are hot.

Best uses—underplantings among trees and shrubs, rock gardens, stream banks. Prefers light shade and moist soil.

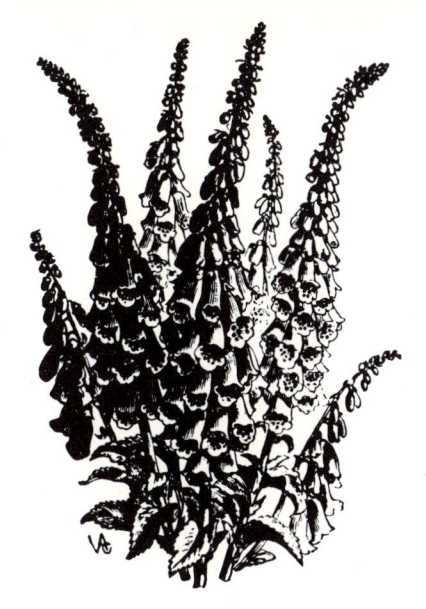

FOXGLOVE
Digitalis purpurea
Mostly perennial;
some biennial plants

Foxglove is a tall, spikey plant like delphinium, and it blends agreeably with other perennials. The colors of foxglove are pastel, and the individual blossoms are often spotted and marked inside. This feature and the characteristic shape of the blossoms give foxglove its quaint name. Foxglove likes to be planted where it will receive afternoon shade, just at the dripline of trees. It also likes the protection from wind that it receives from tall evergreens or a wall. If the trees around your home are still small, plant foxglove against the east side of the house or garage, to keep it in the shade. You can grow it from seeds or started plants. The variety 'Foxy' can bloom the first year from seeds and is considerably shorter than other types.

Blooms continue to form over an extended period. The slender spikes are usually curved and often bowed over at the very tip where new flower buds are forming.

Best uses—excellent for adding the dimension of height to perennial beds. Plant in groups of three to five rather than in rows.

HEMEROCALLIS OR DAYLILY
Hemerocallis
species and cultivars

Put aside any preconceived notions you may have formed as a result of seeing the common tawny daylilies growing in huge clumps along roadsides throughout the East and Midwest. The newer garden cultivars stay within bounds, bloom in myriad shades, and even remain open for most of the day and night. A few talented nurserymen in America have concentrated on improving this versatile flower, and the results have been outstanding!

Daylilies are tough and adaptable; I have seen them blooming merrily from roots thrown on the ash heaps that used to accumulate during coal-burning days. They are hardy —at home from South Texas through New England, depending on the variety involved.

Daylilies form arching clumps to 4 feet or more in diameter, ranging in height from 1½–4 feet (or to 6 feet for cultivars such as 'High

Boy'). Flower stems are long and smooth. Blossoms are numerous on well-established plants. The grass-like leaves are light to medium green. Well-nourished plants will continue to bloom for a month or more during early summer and mid-summer. By planting carefully selected cultivars, you can insure bloom from May through early September. Certain nearly evergreen types for the South and West extend this bloom period.

Daylilies form heavy clumps that rarely need dividing. However, you can increase your holdings of plants by this method. The foliage can be cut back severely after blooming, and the clumps dug and pried out of moist soil with a spading fork. Place the clumps in a shady area and wash the soil off the roots so you can see what you are doing. Pin the clump to the ground with the spading fork, then use a hatchet or cleaver to cut it into smaller clumps, each containing two or three of the fleshy, tuberous roots. Replant the divisions of 4-foot centers. You can minimize transplanting shock by dividing early-blooming sorts in September and the late-blooming kinds in early spring.

Best uses—plant daylilies along paths, among other perennials, or as substitutes for shrubs. Certain cultivars are excellent for cutting. The blossoms come at a convenient time, following bearded iris, when summer annuals have not yet reached their peak.

HOLLYHOCK
Althea rosea.
Perennial, biennial or annual

Many people love hollyhocks but hesitate to plant them because they remember the huge, old-fashioned varieties. Now, tidy 4-foot high varieties are available, adapting hollyhocks even to small gardens where they can be used to fill odd corners and to add height at the ends of fences and walls. The newer varieties bloom in late summer from spring-planted seeds or early the following summer from young plants that live over winter. In rich soil the tall varieties of hollyhock will develop stems as thick as your wrist and 6–8 feet tall. Individual flowers grow as large powderpuffs. They open along the stem as the spike increases in height. Often as many as 2 dozen blossoms of varying maturity can be seen along a spike at one time. Blossoms are fully double, semi-double, or single—frilled and waved; some are bicolored. The color range is tremendous, including some handsome dark burgundy and crimson shades and some near-blue lavender hues.

"Rust disease" is quite prevalent on hollyhocks; at present there are no immune varieties. Plants live through the affects of rust; the disease is more unsightly than lethal. Plant in full sun to decrease the incidence of rust and spray with a fungicide at the first signs of brownish spots on the undersides of leaves. (See the discussion of fungicides on pages 43 and 44.)

Best uses—at the back of annual or perennial borders, as borders along a wide path, or planted in groups of three to five plants in corners. Individual blossoms can be "floated" in water, made into "dolls" for little girls, or strung into leis. The tall spikes, if you can bear to take them from the garden, are handsome when used in tall vases set on the floor.

IRIS
Iris species and cultivars
Perennial

This section will deal mainly with the most popular of the Iris genus—the "tall German or bearded iris." The name is misleading because you can order low-growing cultivars, and the "beard" is a specialized flower part that looks more like a caterpillar than beard. Aside from this, the garden iris is a gem of a plant for display beds and for cutting. Plant breeders have created beautiful colors in blossoms that last for days and days.

The large, perfectly formed blossoms of modern iris cultivars are so exotic that they look out of place in a naturalistic setting. For that reason they are usually grown in special display beds or in rows. Iris grows in clumps from fleshy, knotted, underground stems called rhizomes. The clumps need to be cut apart every two to three years and replanted as divisions. Iris also requires a regular spray program to prevent damage by a serious and widespread pest, the Iris Borer. (Most damage can be prevented if you pull off and burn or haul away the old tops in early spring.)

Of all flowers, probably iris has suffered the most from the misplaced generosity of gardeners who preserve old and inferior cultivars by spreading them among their friends. Consequently, only a few gardeners have enjoyed the glorious creations that breeders have introduced during the decade just past . . delicate, perfect pink, apricot, yellow, lavender, and violet-blue shades; deep, velvety bronze, maroon, and near-black purple. Most iris cultivars are moderately priced. They may be purchased in late summer at garden centers or ordered by mail from a number of commercial growers, mostly in the northwestern states. The newer colors and forms are priced in proportion to the year of introduction, with brand-new, award-winning cultivars bringing impressive prices. Send for catalogs of specialists when you are selecting iris; the color illustrations are fairly accurate, and the descriptions and directions are so complete that they can answer all or most of your questions. Plant rhizomes in the fall. See the section on water plants for Japanese iris, *I. kaempferi*.

Patented cultivars of iris and other vegetatively produced plants should not be grown for sale by other than licensed growers. The breeder can invest years of effort and substantial sums of money in creating an award-winning introduction. The plant patent assures him of protection for a sufficient period of time to allow him to recoup investment and make a profit.

Best uses—cutting, display beds, backgrounds, edgings (use the dwarf cultivars for this purpose).

LILY
Lilium species and hybrids

Much hybridizing of lilies has taken place in recent years, resulting in a wide choice of colors, and of blossom and plant types. Modern lilies range in size from little, bunch-forming, 12-inch-high bedding types to soaring beauties that grow so tall that you must look up at the blossoms. Obviously, with such a variation in height, it is well to read the catalogs carefully.

With lilies it is most important to consider the site in which they are to be planted. For instance, many lilies hang face down from candelabralike sprays. The shorter cultivars of this class display best in a raised bed or on a hillside above a path. The tall lilies look good against a dark backdrop of evergreens or in woodsy glens or ravines. The tall hybrids also show well if planted along a fence where the flower spires show above it. Plant the bulbs in the fall.

Check lily catalog descriptions for mentions of "resistance to mosaic diseases." This virus disease can be transmitted to lily plants by aphids. The species and hybrids that have genetic (inherited) resistance can throw off the effects of the virus, but susceptible types can be stunted or malformed by it. Among the best resistant cultivars are 'Mid-Century Hybrids,' 'Auratum Hybrids,' 'Imperial Hybrids,' and the species *Lilium speciosum*.

Best uses—mixed among perennials in beds or borders for midsummer bloom. The cultivars that grow to less than 3 feet in height make good container plants.

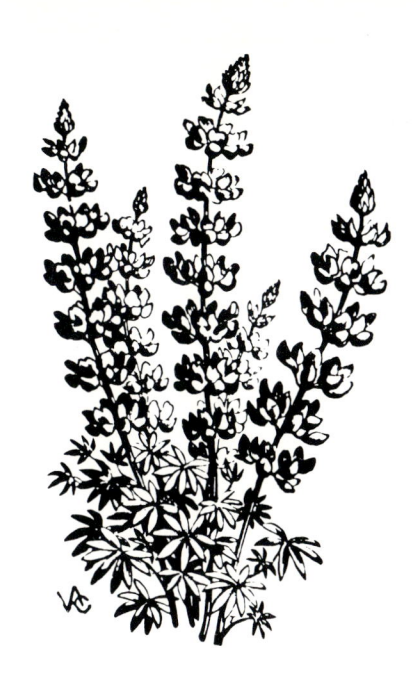

LUPIN
Lupinus
'Russell's and Royal "Hybrids"'
Perennial

An outstanding example of the improvement that can be achieved through plant selection, Russell's and Royal lupins are not F_1 hybrids, but are grown from seeds saved from choice plants.

Wild lupins may be seen carpeting the floor of forests in northern states, blooming among rocks just below timberline on western ranges, or covering road cuts from Texas to California. Yet lupins are not particularly easy to grow in gardens. They prefer well-drained, even gravelly soil, and under the best conditions die out after three or four years. Fortunately, a good mother plant in a favorable location will drop seeds to replace itself many times over.

Garden lupins bloom in early summer; their dense spikes of pea-shaped blossoms are spaced in symmetrical rows. The colors range from deep purple and red through sky blue, pink, and white. Individual blossoms are marked with contrasting pure white or cream. Plants average 29–36 inches in height, taller in the West.

Lupins grow dependably from seeds, but the seeds must be "innoculated." Purchase an inexpensive packet of "Nitragin," "Legume-Aid," or other brand of innoculant and treat the lupin seeds as directed. Innoculants contain spores of a harmless soil bacteria that lupins require for healthy growth. Germination or sprouting will be hastened if you nick the hard, oily coat of lupin seeds with the corner of a triangular file.

Plant in full sun. Lupins aren't happy in the hot, humid south, except at higher elevations.

Best uses—plant in groups among other perennials or at high-interest points in rock gardens.

PEONY OR HERBACEOUS PEONY
Paeonia hybrids
Perennial

Peonies have long been a popular flower. Stroll through a museum and look at some of the florid still lifes; you will see that centuries ago the buxom, pink-cheeked peony blossoms were the center of many flower arrangements.

Plant for plant, few other flowers can match peonies for cut flowers and attractive foliage. The flower stems are long, sturdy, and gratifyingly plentiful. The blooms open before summer annuals have hit their stride. Cultivars are available in various heights, ranging from 18 inches to 4 feet.

Start peonies in late August or early September from tuberous roots. Prepare the soil carefully to at least an 18-inch depth by digging in peat moss (or any other organic soil amendment you have available); a well-prepared bed of peonies can live for 100 years or more. Fertilize peonies after they bloom and again in early fall.

For the most beautiful peonies, secure starts from specialists. White, pink, and crimson colors and bicolors are the most common. Recently introduced hybrids include clear yellow and creamy yellow. The double-flowered types are the most popular, but don't overlook the rain-resistant, single-flowered cultivars; their blossoms look dainty and fragile but make long-lasting cut flowers. The "Japanese" and "anemone" blossom forms have open faces with centers that are tufted or crested.

Peonies require a cold winter to induce the dormancy that is necessary for strong blooms and long life. Peony beds require deep mulching

Petunias edged by alyssum. *Courtesy Ferry-Morse Seed Co.*

Three lilies: 'Imperial Silver,' 'Imperial Crimson,' and 'Imperial Gold.' *Courtesy Oregon Bulb Farms*

'Rainbow Fringed' coleus, mixed colors. *Courtesy T. Sakata & Co.*

Paeonia officinalis

to prevent loss due to heaving where winters are extremely cold.

Best uses—among shrubs and massed in beds among other perennials such as poppies or coral bells. Allow at least 3 feet between large plants. Peonies make choice cut flowers; cut the stems when the flower buds are open about halfway. Leave at least three sets of leaves on the portion of the flower stem remaining on the plant; this prevents depletion of the food reserves within the plant.

PINKS
Dianthus species and cultivars
Perennial, biennial and annual

The huge genus *Dianthus* includes many well-loved hardy perennials and biennials as well as the annuals detailed elsewhere. Many form spreading mats of blue-green, saber-shaped leaves, topped with numerous upright flower stems. Others form upright clumps with stems arching out, fountain-fashion. Peak bloom season is early summer and again in fall (if cut back and fertilized). Most species are sweetly clove scented. The following pinks are those most often used in flower gardens:

MAIDEN PINK
D. Deltoides

Mat-forming groundcover or rock garden species. Small red, purple, and pink blossoms in great profusion. 8–12 inches high, light green foliage.

CARNATION
D. caryophyllus

The garden forms of the florist's carnation grow into medium-sized clumps about 12–24 inches in height. The blossoms are well-formed and about half the size of greenhouse carnations. They make excellent, fragrant cut flowers. Colors include white, pink, rose, salmon, cream, mauve, crimson, and lavender-pink—some have "picotee" markings. Plants are not reliably hardy in northern states and need protection during winter.

CHEDDAR PINK
D. grationapolitanus

Forms distinctive blue-green mounds surmounted by arching stems of small, fragrant pink blossoms. Height: 1 foot.

ROCK PINK
D. neglectus

Plants are mere tufts of green, ideal for chinking into rock gardens, walls, and corners of stone steps. Small pink flowers on 6-inch stems. Long-lived.

COTTAGE PINK OR BORDER PINK
D. plumarius

Summer-blooming pink for edgings; 1 foot high. Fragrant pink, white, or rose blossoms with slightly fringed edges and contrasting centers. Good for cutting. New dwarf cultivars are available.

SWEET WILLIAM
D. barbatus

A most useful biennial for filling in among shrubs, edging borders, or cutting. It volunteers dependably once it has become established. The small flowers are held in flat clusters; flowers are ringed and zoned in contrasting white, red, rose, and pink. Little or no fragrance. The newer dwarf varieties bloom at a height of 6–12 inches; tall varieties reach 24 inches.

SUMMER PHLOX
Phlox paniculata

The backbone of many perennial borders, long-lived summer phlox blooms from June to late August. The plants are many-branched, 2–4 feet high, and come in mostly soft color hues. The upright stems support fluffy spikes of 1-inch-wide flowers.

Grow summer phlox from spring or fall-planted divisions; you may order from a wide range of colors and bicolors, including some delicate pinks and lavenders and unusual salmon-rose shades and pure white. Summer phlox does not come true from seeds; any volunteers that come up should be removed if they sport magenta or faded-pink colors. Place phlox in full sun except in areas where sunlight is very intense. If mildew disease becomes a problem late in summer, begin weekly sprays of fungicide.

MOSS PINK OR CREEPING PHLOX
Phlox subulata

Easterners who exclaim over the glowing mats of groundcover "iceplant" (mesembryanthemum) in California are selling short their own moss pink. It is equally brilliant for spring color, cascading in undulating sheets over rocks, hillocks, and banks. Few other spring flowers have the impact of moss pink with its pink, purple, crimson, lavender-blue, or white colors.

Moss pinks grow into a dense, mossy mat of leaves that blooms in late spring. Trimming, thinning, and feeding after the blossoms have faded helps keep moss pink from getting leggy and dying out. The better colors come from vegetatively reproduced plants.

PLANTAIN LILY OR FUNKIA
Hosta species and cultivars
Perennial

The easy-to-grow plantain lilies are one of the best flowers for shade, and are valued for their broad, handsome, glossy, ribbed leaves. Those with green or blue-green leaves are preferred for naturalistic plantings; the named variegated-leaf cultivars make good conversation plants—they give a dramatic effect, so select their location carefully.

Plantain lilies last for years, slowly spreading into large clumps. Blossom spikes reach 18–36 inches in height. Hostas require moist, fertile soil to hold their foliage color. Treat them well and they will bloom lustily for several weeks during the summer. Blooms of the popular *H. plantaginea* appear in August and are white and fragrant, others have lavender, lilac, or bluish blossoms that come from June through September, depending on the kind. Grow from started plants or vegetative divisions; set plants out in late spring. Plantain lilies thrive in light to dense shade, but blossoms are sparse where sunlight is heavily filtered. (Grow the blue-leaved cultivars in full sun.) Plantain lilies are one of the few plants that can compete successfully with tree roots for water and plant food.

Best uses—groundcovers where trees shade out grass, large containers, poolsides, and other moist spots. For shaded areas, entire borders of plantain lilies are attractive. Cultivars may be mixed in a border if care is taken to place the shorter types in front.

POPPY, ORIENTAL
Papaver orientale
Perennial

Oriental poppies have an open-faced directness and vitality of color and form. The large, cup-shaped blossoms come in strong

Papaver orientale

pink, cerise, orange, white, salmon, watermelon, and scarlet shades. Long, strong stems hold the blossoms high for your approval. Among the open blossoms you will see plump, swan-necked green buds awaiting maturity and their turn to shine. This is the big poppy that is often copied in paper flowers. The petals even have a crinkled, tissue-paper texture to them.

Long-lived oriental poppies may be grown from seeds or fleshy roots, though the choice new colors are not available in seeds. The plants bloom for several weeks beginning in early summer. Plant perennial baby's breath to serve as living markers where oriental poppies grow; in late summer the baby's breath will fill in the empty spaces remaining when the foliage of the poppies withers, shortly after the flowers have faded.

Like peonies, oriental poppies need a sharply cold dormant period. Where they don't receive it, the flower stems are short and the clumps soon die out.

Best uses—mixed with other medium-height perennials. They combine well with fall-blooming asters. which take over when the poppies fade out. Cut for arrangements when buds are just starting to crack open. Seal the cut stems with flame to stop the flow of milky juice. This is not the forbidden "opium poppy.")

SEDUM OR STONECROP
Sedum species
Perennial

These fleshy-stemmed, heat-loving succulents look tender but will come back from roots or seeds year after year in sandy, well-drained rock gardens or rock walls. They tend to spread rather aggressively and should not be planted in or near flower beds where they can become a nuisance. The species with yellow-green foliage are hard to harmonize with other colors in the garden.

Western gardeners can choose from many medium-height, semi-hardy species that have colorful flowers and foliage, but these are not listed here. Instead, only the species that are universally hardy and available are included:

GOLDMOSS SEDUM
S. acre

Low-growing, carpet forming. Small yellow-green leaves, yellow flowers in late spring. Aggressive.

S. lineare
(S. sarmentosum)

Narrow, fleshy, light green leaves. Heavier plants than *S. acre*. Use for hanging baskets and dry walls where its branches can trail.

S. sieboldii

A handsome, trailing plant with flat, thick, notched, blue-green leaves that turn coppery-red in the fall. Large, flat clusters of pink flowers on upright stems in late summer. Rock gardens or hanging baskets.

S. spectabile
"Showy Sedum"

Upright plants, 1 foot or more in height, bear large pink to red flower clusters in early fall. Large, fleshy, blue-green leaves. Good container plant or rock garden specimen for tucking in among boulders where it can bask in the reflected heat.

SHASTA DAISY
Chrysanthemum maximum
Perennial

Upright clumps of shasta daisy brighten up perennial borders with much needed white. One of the few pure white, daisy-flowered perennials for summer and early fall bloom. Easy to grow, except for the occasional digging and dividing required to produce strong new clumps.

The older varieties with small, yel-

Chrysanthemum maximum

low-centered flowers are being superseded by lower-growing cultivars with larger and more interesting doubled or crested blossoms. The more desirable cultivars do not come true from seeds and should be ordered as started plants. Grow shasta daisy in full sun and it will reach a height of 2–2½ feet. In light shade it reaches up higher and the flowers are not as large. Trim or shear off the stems of spent blossoms to keep the clumps in healthy bloom and to maintain blossom size.

Best uses—basic in perennial borders or among shrubs. Excellent for cutting.

SNOW-IN-SUMMER
Cerastium tomentosum
Perennial

Creeping, silvery-gray plants spread to cover rock gardens, walls, and bulb beds with a soft mantle. Snow-in-summer thrives on neglect and under extremes of climate.

Small white flowers on upright stems appear in early summer and last for several weeks, but they are only an added attraction; the tightly knit silver mat of foliage alone is sufficient to justify a place in your garden.

Start in full sun from seeds or small plants. In warm climates the matted plants need to be trimmed, thinned, and fertilized in the late summer to encourage recovery, and the development of volunteer seedlings.

Best uses—Well-drained rock gardens and banks as a groundcover, among spring bulbs, or mixed in clumps with moss pink or sedum.

SWEET PEA, PERENNIAL
Lathyrus latifolius

These long-lived vining plants cover rocks, stumps, low walls, and steep banks (none of which are found in the typical city garden). Country gardeners find perennial sweet peas useful for covering large areas of fertile banks that are too steep to mow and where weeds would otherwise multiply. City gardeners can use perennial sweet peas to soften the lines of wire fences.

Blossoms form in short-stemmed clusters; they are attractive, but not nearly as large nor as colorful as the annual sweet pea. Blossoms are not fragrant. Colors are mostly white and soft pink or deep lavender. Sow seeds in early spring; plants will bloom the first year. More heat-tolerant than the annual types.

Best uses—informal groundcovers or covering low fences.

TICKSEED
Coreopsis grandiflora
Short-lived perennial

If you don't know this flower, imagine a yellow-flowered shasta daisy and you will come fairly close. This 18–30-inch-high summer-flowering perennial blooms right through intense heat and requires very little care. Plants are ordinarily short-lived, but are good about providing replacements that sprout in the shade of the mother plant.

Don't overlook this lively yellow in your color scheme. When you combine coreopsis with the blue summer flowers such as *Salvia farinacae* or with summer forget-me-not (anchusa) you will be pleased every time you look at your garden. Adaptable all over the U.S.A. Blooms the first year from spring-sown seeds. Trim off faded flowers to prolong bloom.

Best uses — perennial borders, long-lasting cut flower with smooth, stiff stems.

VIOLET OR SWEET VIOLET
Viola odorata
Perennial

The "spring violet" need not be the small-flowered, rank-growing plant that is seen as an escaped plant in damp woodlands. Many beautiful colors are now available in 6–10-inch high cultivars that carry the blossoms up where they can be seen . . . rose, pink, and white as well as the traditional violet-blue.

Plant violets **only** where their spreading habit will not cause a problem. They prefer moist soil, woodland shade, or other protection from the hot sun of the afternoon.

Best Uses—groundcover underplantings in woodlands or among large shrubs, or cut flowers for bouquets. The duration of bloom is short for use as edgings and the plants are invasive—reserve violets for naturalizing.

YARROW
Achillea species and cultivars
Perennial

Yarrows can contribute mounds of needed gray-green foliage to unify widely divergent colors in perennial borders or large rock gardens. The popularity of yarrows is largely due to their long-lasting flat flower clusters; they are for arrangements, fresh or dried. The leaves are fernlike and feathery.

Yarrows from seeds are likely to be of the weedy species. The better cultivars from started plants include:

FERNLEAF YARROW
A. filipendulina
'Gold Plate'
Perennial
Tall plants with very large, flat, chrome-yellow flower clusters.
COMMON YARROW
A. millefolium
'Cerise Queen' and
'Fire King'
Red-flowered cultivars from the common white species. Grow to a height of 3 feet.
A. ptarmica
'The Pearl,' 'Perry's White,'
and 'Snowball'
Good, medium-height white flowers for cutting.

Best uses — intersperse plants among clumps of shasta daisies, tickseed, and *rudbeckia*. Cut flowers, drying.

Viola odorata

GLOSSARY

Balanced fertilizer. A mixture of plant nutrient sources containing approximately equal parts of the three major elements: nitrogen, phosphorus, and potash.

Bed. Any area set off for the planting of flowers. A bed may be of any size or shape and may contain only one kind or a number of kinds of flowers.

Bedding flowers. Flower plants grouped in a bed to form a mass of blossom and foliage colors and textures are called "bedding flowers." Bedding flowers may be low-growing or of medium height.

Border. Originally, this term was used to describe rather long, narrow beds bordering on walks, fences, walls, shrub plantings, etc. Now, however, the term "border" has come to be used almost interchangeably with "bed." For this reason the less restrictive term of "bed" has been used, with few exceptions, throughout this book.

Caliche. A whitish soil often seen in the Southwest that is associated with a low average rainfall and is characterized by a high soil pH level and generally low content of organic matter.

Cloche. A glass or plastic cover for a row of plants that hastens growth in cool weather by storing warmth from the sun and by sheltering plants from the wind.

Compost. Properly prepared compost is a brown, nearly odorless product of the decomposition of vegetable (organic) matter with the aid of lime, water, and a small amount of soil. Chemical fertilizers are sometimes added to hasten decomposition and to make it more complete. Occasional aeration of the "compost pile" and frequent additions of water are necessary for the active growth of the soil bacteria and fungi that break down vegetable matter to humus. Compost is used as a soil amendment and serves to make soil more porous and to increase its capacity to store water and plant nutrients.

Cultivar. This modern term is used to describe a named horticultural introduction. Plants within a cultivar

111

are usually quite similar, though not identical, in size, shape, and blossom characteristics. To reduce variation within a cultivar, plants are usually produced by vegetative reproduction *(which see)*. The original mother plant or plants from which a cultivar is increased is called a "clone."

Cultivating the soil. Pulverizing the shallow top layer of soil with a hoe or pronged implement is called "cultivating." Once considered essential to gardening through the creation of a loose "mulch" to reduce evaporation, cultivation is rapidly being superseded by the use of temporary organic mulches or more-or-less permanent mulches of rock fragments, bark, or coarse wood chips.

Deciduous. Woody plants that drop their leaves with the advent of cold fall or winter weather are called "deciduous." The term is not used in conjunction with herbaceous annual or perennial flowers.

Double-flowered. Blossoms that have more than one layer of petals have a "doubled" or "full" appearance. Flowers may be fully double or semi-double, depending on the number of layers of petals.

Dwarf. In plant descriptions "dwarf" means short. Generally, "dwarf" flower plants are less than 12 inches in height at maturity. However, a short-plant selection from a tall variety or cultivar may be called a "dwarf" regardless of its height.

Foliar feeding. Plants can absorb a certain amount of major and minor nutrients through small openings that occur naturally in the surfaces of leaves and stems or of immature bark. Foliar feeding consists of spraying a dilute solution of nutrients on the foliage of plants, where some of it is absorbed. Foliar feeding is generally used in conjunction with conventional fertilizers applied to the soil.

Fungicide. Fungicides are chemicals used to kill or inhibit the growth of disease-causing fungi. They may be in powder form for dusting on plants or in a form that can be dissolved in water for use in sprayers.

Genus; plural, genera. A term used in connection with plants to describe a basic group or category of related plants. Plants within a genus possess similarities, not always obvious, in blossom or leaf construction or arrangement. A genus of plants usually contains several species *(which see)*. When botanical names are used in this book, the name of the genus precedes the species name; for example, *Helianthus annuus*.

Herbaceous. Used to distinguish a plant that does not grow woody or develop bark with age. All annuals and most perennials are herbaceous.

Herbicide. Chemicals used to kill plants. They may be "selective" in their action, killing only selected kinds of plants, or nonselective, killing all growth. "Pre-emergence" herbicides that work by killing seedlings as they sprout also come in selective forms. Herbicides reduce the need for hand weeding in flower and shrub beds. The granular forms are the most convenient.

Hybrid. Federal and state regulations are gradually restricting the use of this term to true first generation "F_1 hybrids" created by controlled crossing of two different plant lines. These genetic combinations create vigorous plants with uniform growth habits and blossom characteristics.

Humus. The near-ultimate breakdown product of the decomposition of vegetable or organic matter is called humus. Peat moss, sawdust, compost, grass clippings, etc., eventually decompose to humus before disappearing from the soil. Humus is composed of dark, very fine particles that can greatly improve garden soils. Beware of the black soil often sold in truckload quantities as "humus"; it often contains quantities of weed seeds.

Killing frost. There are no truly frost-free areas within the continental U.S.A., although killing frosts are rare in parts of southern California and extreme southern Florida. Killing frosts finish off most annual flowers and kill the tops of perennials. The average dates of the last killing frost in the spring and the first killing frost in the fall or winter can be obtained from your County Agent.

Kind. A term that is used rather loosely to describe a group of related plants such as a genus. For example, zinnias are a "kind" and marigolds are a "kind."

Leaching. When water percolates down through soil in gardens or in a container, it picks up metallic ions and salts and carries them down to lower layers or out of the container in drainage water. A certain amount of leaching is necessary; however, in high rainfall areas leaching eventually makes the soil infertile and acid.

Mammalian toxicity. One system of rating the danger of a chemical to man and other mammals. Certain insecticides may be extremely dangerous to handle or to ingest, yet are very short-lived. Others may be relatively safe to handle yet can persist for years, posing a threat to all wildlife as well as man.

Mulch. A layer of coarse particles of organic material, rocks, or sheet plastic is used to conserve garden moisture, aid in water penetration, keep the soil cool, and discourage the growth of weeds. This is mulch. Organic mulches are temporary; they decompose slowly and add humus to the soil; for this reason they require the addition of new material each year or two. Typical organic mulches are wood chips, crushed corncobs, cottonseed, buckwheat, rice, cocoabean, or peanut hulls. "Permanent" mulches of decorative rock or bark chips are generally placed over a layer of sheet plastic; this combination provides the best control of weeds.

Organic matter. Organic matter (not minerals or synthetic chemicals) may be made up of leaves, weeds, grass clippings, or vegetable and flower trimmings from the garden, peat moss or seaweed, or it may be formed from industrial by-products such as sawdust, wood chips, etc.

Peat moss. Peat moss comes in a multitude of bag or bale sizes, colors, particle sizes, and degrees of acidity or alkalinity. German and Canadian peat moss is common in areas near ocean ports; the domestic product predominates elsewhere. Generally, the medium-brown, coarse, slightly acid kinds of peat moss are best for garden use as soil amendments. Peat moss does not make a good mulch because it is reluctant to absorb water when it has dried out. It works best when mixed evenly into 3–6 inches of soil. The coarse kinds of peat moss are also best for potting mixtures; they drain faster than the finely ground material. Peat moss should always be moistened *before* use; it is usually sold in a kiln-dried state that cannot be moistened completely after mixing with the soil.

Peat pots. These little pots of compressed peat moss are most convenient for growing flowers that are to be transplanted to the garden. Plant roots grow right through the walls of the pot, so you simply plant pot and all. It is most important that you cover the rim of the pot with soil when transplanting—otherwise the protruding rim will act as a "wick" and dry out the soil around the roots of the plant. A standard potting mixture of equal parts of sand, loamy soil, and medium-coarse peat moss is used for filling peat pots.

"Perlite," or "Sponge-rok." These are lightweight, white, gritty particles of expanded quartz used as a substitute for soil in rooting cuttings or for general potting up. No plant nutrients are present in these materials, thus cuttings must be fed once they strike roots. These materials are often mixed with medium-coarse peat moss or sphagnum moss for rooting or for seed-flat soil. Expanded quartz drains rapidly and holds just enough water on the particles to meet the needs of plants.

Rooting hormones. Years of use have demonstrated the effectiveness of these chemicals in stimulating the quick and sure formation of roots on leaf and stem cuttings, and in the encouraging of rooting in transplants. They are simple, inexpensive, and safe to use—either as a dust for dipping or as a solution for watering-in transplants.

Seedling. A term generally used to indicate a young plant grown from a seed. Occasionally used specifically to identify a seed-grown offspring of a plant that is usually vegetatively propagated.

Seed. A reproductive body formed by a plant—a baby plant surrounded by food reserve inside several protective layers. A seed may be as small as a grain of dust or as large as a coconut. Not all seeds have the ability to sprout and grow. Their failure may be due to age, high temperatures and humidity, mechanical injury, or damage from insects or diseases.

Single-flowered. Some blossoms have a single layer of petals. These blossoms are usually somewhat larger in diameter than those of double-flowered varieties in the same species.

Sphagnum moss. Natural sphagnum (the "h" is silent) moss comes from bogs in light, greenish-brown, ropy strands. The "milled" form has been shredded for ease in mixing. Sphagnum reputedly contains an unidentified substance that inhibits the growth of microorganisms that could cause diseases and death of seedlings or cuttings. It is an excellent medium for sprouting seeds —either used alone or mixed with expanded quartz. Do not be misled into purchasing "sphagnum peat-moss" in place of true sphagnum moss for starting seeds: the peat moss is a dark brown, dust-fine product formed from the decomposition of sphagnum moss.

Started plants. Commercial growers produce many kinds of started plants for transplanting to the home garden—bedding plants in flats or smaller "market packs"; plants in individual peat, clay, or plastic pots; rooted cuttings. Started plants offer a simple and convenient method of starting a flower garden, albeit a more expensive method than through the use of seeds. It is preferable to purchase started plants that are on the young side, not overgrown or in full bloom.

Systemic insecticides and fungicides. These chemicals provide the most modern method of controlling insects and fungous diseases. They are absorbed into the *system* of plants through the leaves or roots and must be diluted and used precisely as directed to avoid injury to plants. Protection usually lasts for several weeks. Certain systemic poisons have extremely high mammalian toxicity levels; handle them with great care.

Species: plural, species. When used in connection with plants, "species" describes a group of plants resembling each other more than plants in any other group, and all belonging to the same genus. The species name always comes after the genus name, as in *Zinnia elegans*.

Succulents. Succulent plants may be found in a number of genera. All succulents have thick stems or fleshy leaves that serve to store the moisture that can carry the plants safely through long periods of drought. Examples: Sedum and Moss Rose (Portulaca).

"Terralite" or "vermiculite." A shiny, lightweight, granular material produced by expanding the mineral mica. It has the capacity to store large quantities of water and is used alone or mixed with milled sphagnum to sprout seeds and to root cuttings.

"Texture" of foliage. Beginning gardeners often overlook the gross differences in the size, shape, color, and smoothness of leaves of flowers of different sorts. Some are grasslike and smooth, others are large and velvety, still others are tiny and glossy. The overall foliage effect is referred to as "texture." The descriptions of plants rarely tell you enough to allow you to imagine the texture of a plant, thus you have to learn it from actual observation.

True-to-type. Plants within a variety or cultivar should be very similar to each other in blossom and plant habit and color, and should resemble or be "true" to the "type" (the published description). "Off-type" plants are sufficiently dissimilar in one or more characteristics to look out of place in a bed of otherwise true-to-type plants.

Urea and urea-formaldehyde. Urea is a widely available, high-nitrogen, water-soluble fertilizer that is used mostly for lawns. It is too "hot" to be used safely around flowers. Urea-formaldehyde is a relatively safe source of nitrogen that slowly releases its supply of nutrients under the action of soil bacteria. The latter may be used sparingly on flower beds; heavy applications could cause too much vegetative growth at the expense of flowers.

Variety. A term used, in the main, by seedsmen that describes a group of similar plants usually produced from the seeds saved from one superior plant. A certain amount of variation in plant habit and in blossom form and color is unavoidable, yet good seedsmen can produce varieties that are remarkably uniform from plant to plant.

Vegetative production. This process involves the growing of a new plant from a part of an old one. Pieces or whole parts such as roots, leaves, stems, tubers, rhizomes, bulbs, or side sprouts (offsets) may be used. The new plants grow to become very similar to the parent or mother plant, much more so than new plants grown from seeds.

INDEX

Note: Page references in italics indicate illustrations.

Achillea millefolium (yarrow), 60, 109
Achillea ptarmica (yarrow), 60, 109
Adam's needle (*Yucca filamentosa*), 55
Aegopodium podagraria (goutweed), 57
African daisy (*Dimorphotheca sinuata, D. annua, D. pluvialis*), 48, 68–9; *68*
Agapanthus africanus (lily-of-the-Nile), *63*
ageratum (*Ageratum houstonianum*), 48
Ajuga reptans (bugle), 55, 96
allium, giant (*Allium giganteum*), 55
    A. schoenoprasum (chives), 56
Althea rosea (hollyhock), 58, 100
alyssum, *51, 104*
    sweet (*Lobularia maritima*), 16, 48, 69
    hardy (*A. saxatile*, 'Compactum'), 55
amaranthus (*Amaranthus caudatus*), 48; *11, 81*
    A. tricolor (Joseph's coat), 50
amaryllis, giant (*Hippeastrum hybridum*), 62
    A. belladonna (belladonna lily), 62
Anchusa capensis (summer forget-me-not), 53, 60
Anemone
    coronaria 'St. Brigid,' (poppy-flowered anemone), 59
    hupenhensis japonica (Japanese anemone), 58
animal pests, 45
Anthemis tinctoria 'Kelwayi' (golden marguerite), 57
Antirrhinum majus (snapdragon), 53, 79
aphids (plant lice), 42; *41*
Aquilegia (dwarf columbine), 56
Arabis caucasica (wall rock-cress), 60
Armeria maritima (sea-pink), 59
Artemisia
    albula 'Silver King' (wormwood), 61
    frigida (fringed wormwood), 57
Asclepias tuberosa (butterfly-weed), 56

aster
    China (*Callisthephus chinensis*), 48, 81–2; *82*
    cushion (*Aster hybridus nanus*), 55
    New England (*A. novae-angliae*), 55, 94–5; *95*
    New York (*A. novae-belgii*), 94–5
astilbe (*Astilbe*), 65
Aubretia deltoidea (rock-cress), 59
avens (*Geum chiloense*), 55

baby blue-eyes (*Nemophila mensiesii*), 48, 74
    see also cupflower
baby's breath (*Gypsophila elegans*), 14, 18, 48, 69
    G. paniculata, 55
bachelor button, old fashioned (globe amaranth), 50, 86
bachelor's button (*Centaurea cyanus*), 48, 69–70; *69*
balloon flower (*Platycodon grandiflorum*), 55, 95
balsam (*Impatiens balsaminea*), 48; *82*
balsam pear (*Mormodica charantia*), 66
Baptisia australis (false indigo), 57
basil, ornamental (*Ocimum* 'Dark Opal'), 48
basket flower (*Hymenocallis calathina*), 62
basket of gold (*Alyssum saxatile* 'Compactum'), 55
beard tongue (*Penstemon gloxinoides*), 55; *12*
beds, planning of, 16–18; *12, 13, 14, 15*
bee balm (*Monarda* 'Cambridge Scarlet'), 55
bees, 42
beetles, 42
begonias
    fibrous-rooted (*B. semperflorens*), 49, 82–3; *14, 16*
    tuberous-rooted (*B. tuberhybrida*), 62; *20*
belladonna lily (*Amaryllis belladonna*), 62
bells of Ireland (*Molucelia laevis*), 49

Bergenia cordifolia (heartleaf bergenia), 57
bishop's hat (*Epimedium grandiflorum*), 55
bishop's weed (*Aegopodium podagraria*), 57
black-eyed susan vine (*Thunbergia alata*), 66
blanket flower (*Gaillardia pulchella*), 18, 49
    G. aristata, grandiflorum, 55, 95–6; *95*
blazing star (*Liatris pycnostachya*), 55
bleeding heart (*Dicentra spectabilis*), 55, 96
    western (*D. formosa*), 55
blister-cress (*Erysimum asperum*), 55
blue flax (*Linum perenne*), 55
blue lace flower (*Trachymene caerulea*), 49
blue marguerite (*Felecia amelloides*), 62
blue salvia (*Salvia patens*), 59
border pink (*Dianthus plumaris*), 105
Brunnera macrophylla (forget-me-not anchusa), 57
Buddleia davidii (butterfly-bush), 55
bugle(-weed) (*Ajuga reptans*), 55, 96
bulbs, 11, 14, 36, 64; *78*
butterfly-bush (*Buddleia davidii*), 55
butterfly-weed (*Asclepias tuberosa*), 56

caladium (*Caladium bicolor*), 36, 62
Calceolaria crenatiflora (lady's purse), 63
calendula (*Calendula officinalis*), 49, 70
California poppy (*Eschscholzia californica*), 49, 70, 76
calla (*Zantedeschia*), 62
calliopsis (*Coreopsis tinctoria*), 49, 70–1
Calonyction aculeatum (moonflower), 66
Caltha palustris (marsh marigold), 65
Campanula
    carpatica (Carpathian bellflower), 56
    medium calycanthema (Canterbury bells), 56, 96–7; *96*
    persicifolia (peachleaf bluebell), 58
canary bird vine (*Tropaeolum peregrinum*), 66
candytuft (*Iberis umbellata*), 49
    hyacinth flowered (*I. amara*), 49, 71;
    perennial (*I. sempervirens*), 56

canna (*Canna*), 18, 36, 62
Canterbury bells (*Campanula medium calycanthema*), 56, 96–7; *96*
cape marigold (*Dimorphotheca ecklonis*), 62
  see also African daisy
cardinal climber (*Quamlocit pinnata*), 66
cardinal flower (*Lobelia cardinalis*), 64
carnation (*Dianthus caryophyllus*), 105
  see also clove pink; *Dianthus* species
Carpathian bellflower (*Campanula carpatica*), 56
caterpillars, 42
Cantharanthus rosea (Madagascar periwinkle), 52, 89
cattail (*Typha*), 65
celosia (*Celosia plumosa*), 49, *83*
  C. cristata (cockscomb), 49, 83
Centaurea
  cyanus (bachelor's button), 48, 69–70; *69*
  gymnocarpa (dusty miller), 62; *14*
  Cerastium tomentosum (snow-in-summer), 10, 60, 108
cheddar pink (*Dianthus grationapolitanus*), 105
Cheiranthus cheiri (wallflower), 60, 63; *79*
China aster (*Callisthephus chinensis*), 48, 81–2; *82*
Chinese lantern (*Physalis alkekengi*), 56
Chionodoxa (glory-of-the-snow), 64
chives (*Allium schoenoprasum*), 56
Christmas rose (*Helleborus niger*), 56
chrysanthemum (*Chrysanthemum moriflorum*), 24, 56, 97–8; *97*
  coccineum (painted daisy), 68
  frutescens (marguerite), 63
  maximum (Shasta daisy), 60, 107–8; *108*
  parthenium 'White Stars' (feverfew), 62; *14*
clarkia (*Clarkia unguiculata*), 49, 71–2; *72*
  C. amoena (godetia), 50, 71–2
Cleome spinosa (spiderflower), 13, 53; *16*
Clivia miniata (Kafir lily), 63
clove pink (*Dianthus caryophyllus* 'Fragrance'), 62
cockscomb (*Celosia cristata*), 49, 83
coleus (*Coleus blumei*), 22, 24, 49, 83–4; *104*
columbine, dwarf (*Aquilegia alpina*), 56
  long-spurred (*A.* 'Mckana's'), 11, 56, 98
confederate vine (*Antigonon leptopus*), 66
container gardening, 27–8
  use of fertilizers in, 36
Convallaria majalis (lily-of-the-valley), 58
coral bells (*Heuchera sanguinea*), 11, 56; *98*

Coreopsis
  grandiflora 'Sunburst' (tickseed), 60, 108
  tinctoria (calliopsis), 49, 70–1
corms, 11, 14
cornflower (*Centaurea cyanus*), 48, 69–70; *69*
cosmos (*Cosmos bipinnatus*), 18, 49, 84
  yellow (*C. sulphureus*), 50
cottage pink (*Dianthus plumarius*), 105
cranesbill (*Geranium grandiflorum, G. sanguineum*), 56
crocus (*Crocus vernus*), 64
Cucurbita species, 66
cultivating, 13, 27
cupflower (*Nierembergia hippomanica caerulea*), 18, 50
cuttings
  leaf, *23*
  stem, *24* and *n.*
cutworms, 42
cyclamen, florists (*Cyclamen persicum*), 62
Cyperus (umbrella plant), 65
  C. haspan (dwarf papyrus), 65
cypress vine (*Quamlocit pinnata*), 66

daffodils (*Narcissus* species), 64
dahlia (*Dahlia*), 11, 14, 36, 62
"damping off" disease, 22
daylily (*Hemerocallis*), 56, 99–100; *12*
delphinium (*Delphinium*), 10, 24, 56, 98–9; *12, 14*
  annual (*D. grandiflorum*), 50, 72
  D. ajacis (larkspur), 50; *72*
devil-in-a-bush (*Nigella damascena*), 50, 73
Dianthus species
  'Alwoodii' (dianthus), 56
  D. deltoides (maiden pink), 58, 105
  D. caryophyllus 'Fragrance' (clove pink), 62
  see also pink
Digitalis purpurea (foxglove), 57; *99*
Dimorphotheca (African daisy), 48, 68–9; *68*
  D. ecklonis (cape marigold), 62
diseases, plant, 43–4; *43*
Dolichos lablab (hyacinth bean), 66
Doronicum caucasicum 'Magnificum' (leopard's bane), 58
dusting, 44–5; *44*
dusty miller (*Centaurea gymnocarpa*), 62; *14*
Dutch crocus, 64

earwigs, 42
Echinops exaltatus (globe thistle), 57
Echium fastuosum (pride of Madeira), 63
English daisy (*Bellis perennis*), 57
Epimedium grandiflorum (bishop's hat), 55
Eranthis (winter aconite), 64
Eremurus himalaicus (foxtail lily), 62

Eryngium amethystinum (sea-holly), 59
Erysimum asperum (blister-cress), 55
Euphorbia
  myrsinites (myrtle euphorbia), 58
  veneta (*wulfenii*), 57
European pasque-flower (*Anemone pulsatilla*), 57

false dragon head (*Physostegia virginiana*), 57
false indigo (*Baptisia australis*), 57
false spirea (*Astilbe*), 65
feeding, plant, 22–3, 28, 36
  see also fertilizers
fernleaf yarrow (*Achillea filipendulina*), 57, 109
fertilizers, 34–5; *33, 34, 35*
feverfew (*Chrysanthemum parthenium* 'White Stars'), 62; *14*
floss flower (ageratum), 48
flowering tobacco (*Nicotiana alata, N. sanderae*), 50; *84*
forget-me-not (*Myosotis sylvatica, M. scorpiodes*), 50, 99
  anchusa (*Brunnera macrophylla*), 57
  'blue bird' biennial, 57
four o'clock (*Mirabilis jalapa*), 50, 84–6
foxglove, common, 'Excelsior' (*Digitalis purpurea*), 57; *99*
  dwarf 'Foxy' (*D. purpurea* hybrid), 57
foxtail lily (*Eremurus himalaicus*), 62
freesia, hybrids (*Freesia*), 62
fringed wormwood (*Artemisia frigida*), 57
fuchsias, 28

Gaillardia
  pulchella (blanket flower), 18, 49
  aristata grandiflorum (blanket flower), 55, 95–6; *95*
Galanthus (snowdrops), 64
gayfeather (*Liatris pycnostachya*), 55
gazania (*Gazania parviflora* 'Copper King'), 62
Gentiana asclepiadea (willow gentian), 61
geranium (*Pelargonium hortorum*), 24 and *n.*, 86; *16, 20*
  'Lady Washington' (*P. domesticum*), 63
  ivy (*P. peltatum*), 36
gerbera (*Gerbera jamesonii*), 62
geum (*geum chiloense*), 55
gladiolus (*Gladiolus hortulanus*), 11, 16
globe amaranth (*Gomphrena globosa*), 50; *86*
globe-flower (*Trollius europaeus*), 57
globe thistle (*Echinops exaltatus*), 57
gloriosa daisy (*Rudbeckia* hybrid), 50, 87; *34*
glory lily (*Gloriosa rothschildiana*), 63

117

glory-of-the-snow (*Chionodoxia*), 64
godetia (*Clarkia amoena*), 50, 71–2
golden marguerite (*Anthemis tinctoria* 'Kelwayi'), 57
gourds, ornamental (*Cucurbita* species), 66
goutweed (*Aegopodium podagraria*), 57
grape hyacinth (*Muscari*), 64
grasshoppers, 42
groundcovers, 11; *16, 17*
Gypsophila elegans (baby's breath), 14, 18, 48, 69
gypsum, 32–3

hardening off, 24
heartleaf bergenia (*Bergeneoia cordifolia*), 57
Helianthus annuus (sunflower), 53; *91*
Helichrysum bracteatum (strawflower), 53
heliopsis (*Heliopsis scabra*), 57
Helenium autumnale (sneeze-weed), 60
heliotrope (*Heliotropum arborescens*), 63
Helleborus niger (Christmas rose), 56
hens and chickens (*Sempervivum tectorum*), 57
Hesperis matronalis (sweet rocket), 60
Heuchera sanguinea (coral bells), 11, 56; *98*
hibiscus (*Hibiscus moscheotus*), 65
Hippeastrum hybridum (giant amaryllis), 62
hollyhock (*Althea rosea*), 58, 100
hyacinth (*Hyacinthus*), 14, 64
hyacinth bean (*Dolichos lablab*), 66
Hymenocallis calathina (basket flower), 62

Iceland poppy (*Papaver nudicaule*), 63, 76–7
"ice plant" (*Mesembryanthemum*), 106
impatiens (*Impatiens sultani, I. holstii*), 22, 24, 28, 50, 87
  I. balsaminea (balsam), 48; *82*
Indian shot (*Canna*), 18, 36, 62
insect pests, 29, 41–3, 101
insecticides, 42–3
  see also spraying and dusting
Ipomea purpurea (morning glory), 66
iris
  bearded or German (*Iris pogoniria*), 11, 58, 100–2; *19, 101*
  Japanese (*I. Kaempferi*), 65, 102
  reticulata (*I. reticulata*), 64
  Siberian (*I. siberica*), 65
irish moss (*Sagina subulata, Arenaria verna caespitosa*), 58

Japanese anemone (*Anemone hupenhensis japonica*), 58
Japanese spurge (*Pachysandra terminalis*), 58

Joseph's coat (*Amaranthus tricolor*), 50

Kafir lily (*Clivia miniata*), 63
Kniphofia uvaria (red hot poker), 63
kochia, 13

lady's purse (*Calceolaria crenatiflora*), 63
larkspur (*Delphinium ajacis*), 50; *72*
Lathyrus odoratus (sweet pea), 53, 79–80; *34, 80*
lavender (*Lavandula spica*), 58
leaf hoppers (white flies), 42
leopard's bane (*Doronicum caucasicum* 'Magnificum'), 58
Leucojum (snowflake), 64
Liatris pycnostachya (blazing star), 55
lily (*Lilium*), 11, 18, 58; *12, 14, 16, 102, 104*
  L. canadense (meadow lily), 65
lily-of-the-Nile (*Agapanthus africanus*), 63
lily-of-the-valley (*Convallaria majalis*), *58*
lily turf, big blue (*Liriope muscari*), 63
lime, 32–3
Limonium latifolium (sea-lavender), 59
Linum
  grandiflorum rubrum (scarlet flax), 53
  perenne (blue flax), 55
lobelia (*Lobelia erinus*), 10, 18, 28, 50
  L. cardinalis (cardinal flower), 64
lotus (*Nelumbo*), 65
love-in-a-mist (*Nigella damascena*), 50, 73
love-lies-bleeding (*Amaranthus caudatus*), 48; *11, 81*
lupin
  annual (*Lupinus hartwegii*), 52
  perennial (*L.* 'Russell's'), 58, 103
  L. tricolor elegans, 103
Lychnis coronaria (mullein pink), 58
lythrium (*Lythrium salicaria*), 65

Madagascar periwinkle (*Catharanthus rosea*), 52, 89
maiden pink (*Dianthus deltoides*), 58, 105
manure, 32; poultry, 36
marguerite (*Chrysanthemum frutescens*), 63
marigold, 10, 18, 29; *9, 16, 20; 85*
  African or American (*Tagetes erectus*), 52, 87–8; *87*
  French (*Tagetes patula*), 52, 88–9; *88*
marsh marigold (*Caltha palustris*), 65
marvel of Peru (*Mirabilis jalapa*), 50, 84–6
Matthiola incana (stock), 53, 79
matricaria (feverfew), 62; *14*
maypop (*Passiflora incarnata*), 66
meadow lily (*Lilium canadense*), 65
meadow sweet (*Astilbe*), 65
Mexican sunflower (*Tithonia rotundifolia*), 52
Mexican zinnia, *85*

Michaelmas daisy (*Aster novae-angliae*), 55, 94–5; *95*
micronutrients, 36
midges, 42
mignonette (*Reseda odorata*), 52
Mirabilis jalapa (four o'clock) 50, 84–6
mites, 42
Molucelia laevis (bells of Ireland), 49
Monarda 'Cambridge Scarlet' (bee balm), 55
money plant (*Lunaria*), 10
moonflower (*Calonyction aculeatum*), 66
Mormodica charantia (balsam pear), 66
morning glory (*Ipomea purpurea*), 66
moss pink (*Phlox subulata*), 59, 106
moss rose (*Portulaca grandiflora*), 52
mountain garland (*Clarkia unguiculata*), 49, 71–2; *72*
mourning bride (*Scabiosa atropurpurea*), 52
mulches, 27, 28–9
mullein pink (*Lychnis coronaria*), 58
Muscari (grape hyacinth), 64
Myosotis sylvatica (forget-me-not), 50, 99
myrtle euphorbia (*Euphorbia myrsinites*), 58

Narcissus species, (daffodils), 64
nasturtium (*Tropaeolum majus*), 10, 52, 72
Nelumbo (lotus), 65
nemesia (*Nemesia strumosa*), 52; *73*
Nemophila mensiesii (baby blue-eyes), 48, 74
Nicotiana alata, N. sanderae (flowering tobacco), 50; *84*
Nigella damascena (love-in-a-mist), 50, 73

Ocimum 'Dark Opal' (ornamental basil), 48
Oenothera
  erythrosepala, lamarckiana (evening primrose), 59
  speciosi childsii (Mexican primrose), 59

Pachysandra terminalis (Japanese spurge), 58
painted daisy (*Chrysanthemum coccineum*), 58
painted tongue (*Salpiglossis sinuata*), 52
pansy (*Viola tricolor hortensis*), 10, 29, 52; *74*
Papaver
  nudicaule (Iceland poppy), 63, 76–7
  oriental (oriental poppy), 59, 106–7; *107*
  rhoeas (shirley poppy), 53; *77*
papyrus, dwarf (*Cyperus haspan*), 65
passion flower (*Passiflora incarnata*), 66
peachleaf bluebell (*Campanula persicifolia*), 58
peat moss, 28, 32
peony (*Paeonia*), 16, 58, 103–5; *19, 105*

petunia (*Petunia hybrida*), 10, 52, 89–90; *17, 34, 89, 104*
pH, 37
Phaseolus coccineus (scarlet runner bean), 66
phlox
    annual (*Phlox drummondi*), 52, 75; *75, 76*
    blue (*P. divaricata*), 57
    creeping (*P. subulata*), 59, 106
    perennial (*P. paniculata*), 10, 16, 59; *106*
Physalis alkekengi (Chinese lantern), 56
Physostegia virginiana (false dragon head), 57
pickerelweed (*Pontederia*), 65
picking off, 29
pincushion flower (*Scabiosa atropurpurea*), 52
    perennial (*S. caucasica*), 59
pink (*Dianthus* species), 53, 105
    carnation (*D. caryophyllus*), 105
    cheddar pink (*D. grationapolitanus*), 105
    clove pink (*D. Caryophyllus* 'Fragrance',) 62
    cottage or border pink (*D. plumarius*), 105
    D. chinensis, 76; *13*
    maiden pink (*D. deltoides*), 105
    rock pink (*D. neglectus*), 105
    sweet william (*D. barbatus*), 10, 60, 105
plantain-lily, fragrant (*Hosta plantaginea, subcordata*), 59, 106
    variegated (*H. decorata*), 59
"planting well," *28*
Platycodon grandiflorum (balloon flower), 55, 95
poisons, garden, 45–6
pollution damage to plants, 45
polygonum, dwarf, *17*
Pontederia (pickerelweed), 65
poppy
    Iceland (*Papaver nudicaule*), 63, 76–7
    oriental (*P. oriental*), 59, 106–7; *107*
    shirley (*P. rhoeas*), 53; *77*
poppy-flowered anemone (*Anemone coronaria* 'St. Brigid'), 59
poppy mallow (*Callirhoe involucrata*), 59
Portulaca grandiflora (moss rose), 52
pot marigold (*Calendula officianalis*), 49, 70
pride of Madeira (*Echium fastuosum*), 63
primrose
    English (*Primula polyantha*), 59
    evening (*Oenethera erythrosepala, lamarckiana*), 59
    Mexican (*O. speciosa childsii*), 59

Quamlocit pinnata (cardinal climber), 66

ranunculus, Persian (*Ranunculus asiaticus*), 63
red hot poker (*Kniphofia uvaria*), 63
Reseda odorata (mignonette), 52
rhizomes, 11, 14, 100
rock-cress (*Aubretia deltoidea*), 59
rock pink (*Dianthus neglectus*), 105
rosa de montana (*Antigonon leptopus*), 66
roses, 11, 14; *16*
Rudbeckia hybrid (gloriosa daisy), 50, 87; *34*

Sagina subulata (irish moss), 58
Salpiglossis sinuata (painted tongue), 52
salvia (*Salvia splendens*), 13, 18, 53; *16, 90*
    blue (*S. farinaciae*), 90
    gentian (*S. patens*), 59
salvinia (*Salvinia*), 65
sand, 28
sawdust, composted, 28, 32
saxifrage 'London Pride' (*Saxifraga umbrosa*), 59
Scabiosa atropurpurea (pincushion flower), 52
scarlet flax (*Linum grandiflorum rubrum*), 53
scarlet runner bean (*Phaseolus coccineus*), 66
"Scatter Garden Mixtures," 77
scilla (*Scilla*), 64
sea-holly (*Eryngium amethystinum*), 59
sea-lavender (*Limonium latifolium*), 59
sea-pink (*Armeria maritima*), 59
Sedum
    linearum (*S. armentosum*), 107
    sieboldii (stonecrop), 60, 107; *12*
    spectabile (showy sedum), 60, 107
Sempervivum tectorum (hens and chickens), 57
Shasta daisy (*Chrysanthemum maximum*), 60, 107–8; *108*
showy sedum (*Sedum spectabile*), 60, 107
Siberian wallflower (*Erysimum asperum*), 55
signet marigold (*Tagetes signata*), 54
"slips," *24* and *n.*
slugs, 25, 29, 42
snails, 25, 29, 42
snapdragon (*Antirrhinum majus*), 53, 79; *51, 85*
sneeze-weed (*Helenium autumnale*), 60
sneezewort (*Achillea ptarmica* 'Perry's White'), 60, 109
snowdrops (*Galanthus*), 64
snowflake (*Leucojum*), 64
snow-in-summer (*Cerastium tomentosum*), 10, 60, 108
soils, 36–40
squill (*Scilla*), 64

speedwell (*Veronica*), 60
sphagnum moss, 21, 22; *28*
spiderflower (*Cleome spinosa*), 13, 53; *16*
sponge rock, 2o
squash bugs, 42
statice (*Limonium sinuata, L. bonduellii*), 53
starting seeds
    indoors, 21–3; *21, 22*
    in garden, 25–7; *26*
spraying and dusting, 44–5; *44*
stock (*Matthiola incana*), 53, 79
Stokes' aster (*Stokesia laevis*), 60
stonecrop (*Sedum sieboldii*), 60, 107; *12*
strawflower (*Helichrysum bracteatum*), 53
sultana (*Impatiens sultani*), 22, 24, 28, 50, 87
summer forget-me-not (*Anchusa capensis*), 53, 60
summer lilac (*Buddleia davidii*), 55
sunflower (*Helianthus annuus*), 53; *91*
swamp mallow (*Hibiscus moscheotus*), 65
sweet pea (*Lathyrus odoratus*), 53, 79–80; *34, 80*
    perennial (*L. latifolius*), 60, 108
sweet rocket (*Hesperis matronalis*), 60
sweet violet (*Viola odorata*), 60, 108–9; *109*
sweet william (*Dianthus barbatus*), 10, 60, 105

tagetes (*Tagetes tenuifolia, signata*), 54
    T. erectus (African or American marigold), 52, 87–8; *87*
    T. patula (French marigold), 52, 88–9; *88*
thermopsis (*Thermopsis caroliniana*), 60
thrips, 42
Thunbergia alata (black-eyed susan vine), 66
tickseed (*Coreopsis grandiflora* 'Sunburst'), 60, 108
Tithonia rotundifolia (Mexican sunflower), 52
tomatoes, dwarf, 282
tools, garden, 30–1
torch lily (*Kniphofia uvaria*), 63
Torenia fournieri (wishbone flower), 54
touch-me-not (*Impatiens balsaminea*), 48; *82*
Trachymene caerulea (blue lace flower), 49
transplanting
    indoors, 23
    to the garden, 24–5
Transvaal daisy (*Gerbera jamesonii*), 62
trillium (*Trillium*), 64
Trollius europaeus (globe-flower), 57
Tropaeolum
    majus (nasturtium), 10, 52, 72
    peregrinum (canary bird vine), 66
tubers, 11, 14

tufted pansy (*Viola tricolor hortatensis*), 10, 29, 52; *74*
tulip (*Tulipa*), 11, 14, 64
Typha (cattail), 65

umbrella plant (*Cyperus*), *65*

verbena (*Verbena hybrida*), 54, 91–2; *16, 91*
Vinca rosea, 89; *89*
vines, flowering, 11, 66
viola (*Viola cornuta*), 54, 74
    V. odorata (sweet violet), 60, 108–9; *109*
    V. tricolor hortensis (pansy), 10, 29, 52; *74*
violet-scented iris (*Iris reticulata*), 64
Virginia bluebells (*Mertensia virginica*), *60*

wakerobin (*Trillium*), 64
wallflower (*Cheiranthus cheiri*), 60, 63; *79*
wall rock-cress (*Arabis caucasica*), 60
water and bog plants, 11, 65
water lily (*Nymphaea*), 65; *17*
watering, 12, 22; *25*
wax begonias (*Begonia semperflorens*), 49, 82–3; *14, 16*
weeding and cultivating, 13, 27
willow gentian (*Gentiana asclepiadea*), 61
winter aconite (*Eranthis*), 64
winter cleanup, 29
wishbone flower (*Torenia fournieri*), 54
wormwood (*Artemisia albula* 'Silver King'), 61

yarrow
    Achillea millefolium 'Fire King,' 60, 109
    A. ptarmica 'Perry's White,' 60, 109
    fernleaf (*A. filipendulina*), 57, 109
Yucca filamentosa (Adam's needle), 55

Zantedeschia (calla), 62
zinnia (*Zinnia elegans, Z. angustifolia*), 18, 29, 54, 92; *85, 93*